Jane Butel's

Finger Lickin' Rib Stickin' Great Tasting Hot and Spicy

BARBECUE

TURNER
PUBLISHING COMPANY

Turner Publishing Company
Nashville, Tennessee
New York, New York
www.turnerpublishing.com

Jane Butel's Finger Lickin', Rib Stickin', Great Tastin', Hot and Spicy Barbecue

Cover design: Maddie Cothren
Book design: Mallory Collins

Library of Congress Cataloging-in-Publication Data

Names: Butel, Jane.
Title: Jane Butel's finger lickin', rib stickin', great tasting, hot and
  spicy barbecue.
Other titles: Finger lickin', rib stickin', great tastin', hot & spicy
  barbecue | Finger lickin', rib stickin', great tasting, hot and spicy
  barbecue
Description: Nashville, Tennessee : Turner Publishing Company, [2017] |
  Previous edition published under title: Finger lickin', rib stickin',
  great tastin', hot & spicy barbecue / by Jane Butel ; illustrations by
  Jerry Joyner. | Includes index.
Identifiers: LCCN 2017018894 | ISBN 9781681624761 (pbk. : alk. paper)
Subjects: LCSH: Barbecuing. | LCGFT: Cookbooks.
Classification: LCC TX840.B3 B87 2017 | DDC 641.7/6--dc23
LC record available at https://lccn.loc.gov/2017018894

Printed in the United States of America
16 17 18 19 20 10 9 8 7 6 5 4 3 2 1

To all my closest . . . friends, cooking school
students, foodies, and all who just love goopy, spicy,
wonderfully flavored smoked meats and veggies.

ACKNOWLEDGMENTS

To dig up, create, and develop this act of love, I truly thank
all who helped develop the first edition and all who helped
dig up those favorite pit stops throughout our whole US of A!

CONTENTS

BARBECUE ANYTIME • 1

BARBECUE BASICS • 5

OUTDOOR BARBECUE • 13
Jane's Best Barbecued Ribs • 14
James Beal's Barbecued Ribs • 15
Super-Secret Baby Back Pork Ribs • 16
Fiery Hot and South Carolina Pork • 18
"BBCs" (Beer Barbecued Pork Chops) • 19
Hamburgers Made Special • 20
New Mexico Barbecued Beef Ribs • 21
Terry Johnson's Hawaiian Luau Barbecued Beef Ribs • 22
Alabama Smoky Barbecued Chicken • 24
Sunny Arizona's Special Chicken • 26
Jerry Wood's Personal Favorite Barbecued Chicken • 27
Anthony's Sicilian Barbecued Chicken • 28
Southwest Chicken BBQ • 29
Outrageous Ham Steak • 30
Down Home Louisiana Barbecued Shrimp • 31
Florida Shrimp • 32

INDOOR BARBECUE • 33
Barbecued Pork • 34
Bernie's Asian Ribs • 35

Barbecued Country-Style Pork Ribs • 36

New England Maple Barbecued Pork • 37

Yankee Brisket Pulled Barbecue • 38

Pulled Barbecue • 39

Texas Beef Barbecue • 40

Amy's Sloppy Joe's • 41

Jerry's Beef Barbecue • 42

Jane's Special Sweet and Sour Chicken • 43

Sweet Southern Chicken • 44

Addie's Texas Barbecued Chicken • 45

Orange Barbecued Ham • 46

Mustard Barbecued Ham • 47

Steve's Bermuda Lamb • 48

Big Fish Barbecue • 49

San Francisco Barbecued Fish • 50

ACCOMPANIMENTS • 51
Chuckwagon Salad • 52

Kay's Lexington Barbecue Coleslaw • 53

Texas Potato Salad • 54

Barbecued Baked Beans • 55

Corn on the Cob • 56

Barbecued Cheese • 56

Norma Jean's Hush Puppies • 57

Fudge Cake • 58

Texas Pecan Cake • 59

PIT STOPS • 61

INDEX • 81

Barbecue Anytime

Barbecue . . . Bar-B-Que . . . Bar-B-Q . . . Barbeque. The passions generated by this gutsy American dish, no matter how you spell it, are real, although hardly anyone agrees just what barbecue is all about. The answer is far from clear cut and depends on your definition of *barbecue*. To some it means a spicy sauce, to others a cooking style; then there are those who say it's a drippy meat concoction, and to anyone with a backyard it's a festive outdoor party.

Barbecue, as I speak of it in this book, is the saucy stuff with a smoky taste. *Stuff* here means almost any kind of meat; *sauce* means a collection of the best-tasting, finger-licking, zesty combinations found in this country and given to me by some of America's finest barbecue cooks.

Some recipes originally called for pit-smoked meats, but all have been adapted for home use. And because great barbecue was developed through lots of improvisation, you can continue the tradition—prepare it outdoors on a grill or in a smoker, or indoors on top of the range, in the oven, or under the broiler.

Pit Smoking

The style of cooking meats over an open fire pit has been around since the days of the Peking Man. Many Southern barbecue lovers still consider pit smoking the best method for preparing barbecued meat. There's never been one specific design set-up for a pit, but when I was a child you always began with a very large hole about six feet across and four feet deep. Then a layer of heat-resistant rocks was added. A heavy mesh screen was put down over the rocks, then on top went a layer of hardwood such as hickory, oak, alder, or fruit wood. Once the fire got going and the white hardwood coals remained, the prepared meat (the whole skinned animal) was lowered into the pit on a spit and the pitmasters, as the fire tenders were called, used their own carefully guarded secret techniques for getting moist, smoky, succulent results. A good pitmaster was a genius at controlling the low heat for the sixteen hours necessary for the meat drippings to flavor the smoke which, in turn, enriched the smoky taste of the meat.

Nowadays, it's harder to find real outdoor pit barbecue. And pit-cooked no longer necessarily means that the meat had been lovingly tended and basted for hours at a stretch. Also, various states have very stringent laws governing open pits. Consequently many fine barbecue restaurants and all commercial barbecue manufacturers use gas- or electric-fired equipment to control temperatures and conditions. A few landmark restaurants, a number of which are featured in the "Pit Stops" section, use real open pits. And, of course, each of the owners is proud of his or her accomplishment.

Pork shoulders, butts and spareribs are the most popular meats to pit smoke. Once smoked, shoulders and butts are sold "pulled" and partially "pulled." Popularized and most prevalent in the South, "pulled" indicates that the cooked meat has been separated along the grain into shreds with forks or by hand before the sauce is added. Partially "pulled" means that the meat has been partially separated, then cut into one- inch chunks or strands. Beef is also pit cooked, but requires moister heat than pork. This can be simulated in home methods by tightly covering the cut of meat with a lid or aluminum foil.

SMOKEHOUSE BARBECUING

Smokehouse cooking came along much later than pit smoking and in the US it became popular further north and west. Weather conditions made it a less risky way of smoking meat. It was used to slowly remove moisture from the meat and flavor it at the same time. This procedure was also invaluable for extending the life of the meat. Pork shoulders, butts and ribs are all smoked this way.

Not too many years ago, a smokehouse was simply a large house surrounded with outside pits where hardwood fires were closely watched until the fire burned down to hot coals. The wood chips (presoaked in water overnight) were thrown onto the coals which in turn created a large volume of smoke. The smoke was vented into the smokehouse and smoked the meat.

The meat fat does not drip onto the fire, so smokehouse barbecue tastes different from pit-smoked barbecue. The carbonized charcoal taste is not produced, resulting in a more subtly smoky, drier product which eliminates "pulled" barbecue from the realm of possibility in smokehouse smoking. Each system has its following and most devotees, like myself, love both.

FINGER LICKIN' BARBECUE

Along with great meat preparation, for most of us a successful barbecue ultimately is determined by how delicious the sauce used to marinate, baste, or accompany the meat tastes.

I am convinced that the lack of information on the origins of this saucy American barbecue—spicy, savory, and lip-smacking fabulous—stems from the fact that over the years, no one thought of writing down their recipes. Eventually, when recipe-writing developed as a way of sharing formulas for favorite tastes, regional secrets were so jealously guarded that rather than share recipes indiscriminately they were passed on verbally and through demonstration to only the most trusted individuals. This method gave rise, especially in the Southeast and Southwest, to the pitmaster or master barbecuer who was known to exist in most every county during the 1800s.

Each region of the deep South developed definite formulas for barbecue, so today, in some parts of South Carolina and southern Texas, vinegar bastes are used and the sauce is put on after the meat is cooked. In other parts of South Carolina, mustard sauces abound. Further north and east, tomato-base sauces prevail. Sweet, thick, ketchup-base sauces crop up in family formulas throughout the Southwest, some smoky, some not; some hot as fire, others mild. And even to this day in the hardwood forested areas of the Carolinas, Alabama and southeast Texas, good, old-fashioned pits are still used to smoke meats.

THE BACKYARD BARBECUE

In searching for the origins of barbecue as a backyard event, a story came to my attention in an article written by Orin Anderson entitled "The Quest for the Best Barbecue in the World," published in South Carolina's *Sandlapper* magazine in July 1979. It seems a couple of hundred years ago (or so) a wealthy man named Bernard Quayle decided to throw a get-together for several hundred special friends. Everyone loved it so much that he repeated the event again and again. The food served at these feasts consisted of whole sheep, hogs, and steers, roasted over pits. The guests ate this sumptuous feast at long tables set outdoors. Mr. Quayle was not the only rancher to entertain in this fashion, but his parties were so extensive and unusual that the name of his ranch became an expression for pit cooking and outdoor eating: The—(Bar) BQ.

You don't need fancy equipment to enjoy barbecue. Although many of the recipes suggest cooking outdoors on a grill, all can be prepared indoors if you have no backyard or if the weather turns ugly. The sauces used for each dish are listed separately in almost every recipe. They can be made in advance and refrigerated or even frozen. Keep favorites on hand for emergencies—unexpected company, for instance—or to liven up an otherwise dull dish.

Think of barbecue for any season and any time. Remember, you don't need to own a barbecue to throw a barbecue and to serve barbecue!

BARBECUE BASICS

Although you may want to go crazy with your newfound barbecue pleasures, don't go hog wild at the beginning. A few simple tools will get you started, and they don't need to be expensive. You can get more sophisticated equipment if you want, but remember, you can get good barbecue flavor with even the most basic equipment, including your oven broiler. Experimentation is the only real way to master your barbecue technique.

GRILLS

The best bet for the barbecue novice is a small brazier or lightweight folding grill. Both are inexpensive and easy to store. If you want to purchase a more elaborate model, my choice among these variations would always be a grill with a lid. It will give the food that special smoky flavor, which is well worth the extra few minutes of cooking time.

You can adapt an open brazier grill by making a foil tent, using heavy-duty broiler foil (see page 25), to sit over the food as it cooks on the grill and function like a lid.

If you get a new grill, don't discard your old one, however, because you can use it for appetizers, breads, and side dishes while the meat cooks on the other one, and you can also store hot coals in it for prolonged cooking on the main grill.

Every type of grill works a little differently. To get the most out of yours, read the manufacturer's instructions thoroughly before using it.

BRAZIER GRILLS The most popular, lightweight, and inexpensive, these grills range from simple tabletop units to models on wheels with hoods and rotisseries. Larger versions have cranks to adjust the grill height, which aids in controlling cooking temperatures.

HIBACHIS These small, efficient, cast-iron open grills have adjustable grates, air dampers, and coal racks to allow the ashes to fall to the bottom. Perfectly sized for appetizers, small kebobs, and barbecue for two.

KETTLE AND WAGON GRILLS These versatile grills are more expensive. Both types feature lids. Air dampers in the bottom of the grill and in the lid control ventilation and thereby the cooking temperature. When open they function like brazier grills; when closed they work like ovens with the heat controlled by the dampers. You can give the meat a smoked quality by simply adding damp hickory chips to the hot coals and closing the lid.

GAS AND ELECTRIC GRILLS These grills both work on the radiant-heat principle. Volcanic pumice or ceramic briquettes are placed on racks between the heat source and the grill. Then the heat from the briquettes cooks the food. These grills are extra-convenient versions of the kettle or wagon models; they are easier to start and have more efficient heat control. But for the tastiest results, I prefer cooking over hardwood briquettes to gas or electric grills.

TESTING THE CHARCOAL

One way to test the temperature of the fire is to place the palm of your hand above the coals at the approximate level the food will be cooking:

    3 inches for beef and lamb
    4 inches for poultry
    5 inches for pork

If you can hold your palm steady for

    3 seconds, the fire is ready to cook.
    4 seconds, the fire is medium hot (350°F, 175°C) and
        you can still start your meat at this temperature.
    5 seconds or more, the fire is too cool to use yet.

To raise the temperature, knock the ash from the briquettes and push them closer together. You might also try fanning with a bellows or a folded newspaper. To lower the temperature, distribute the coals farther apart, raise the grill, or mist with water.

BRIQUETTES

Charcoal briquettes come in two types. Hardwood briquettes are made by burning down oak, hickory, or other hardwoods under controlled heat until they are completely charred. Then they are compressed by a machine into briquettes. Coal briquettes are cheaper, but I don't recommend them—you won't get that great smoky taste.

Prepare your charcoal by piling it in a mound in the bottom of the grill, then start your fire. You will need a minimum of 36 briquettes for 3 to 6 pounds of chicken or ribs. If you are barbecuing a roast, add a dozen briquettes for each additional 2 pounds of weight above 3 pounds. After 30 to 45 minutes, when the coals are coated with white ash, use a long-handled fork or poker to knock off the ash (which traps the heat inside each briquette).

Spread the coals out evenly in the firebox. It is important to have a spray bottle handy, filled with water for spritzing the coals to produce smoke and to douse flames, as well as long-handled implements and fireproof mitts. By the way, it isn't the flame that cooks the meat; it's the direct infrared radiation from completely heated coals.

Charcoal and wood fires take 30 to 40 minutes to burn down to the ash-covered coals needed for grilling. Outdoor gas cookers take 10 minutes to warm up. Electric grills take approximately 25 minutes.

Position the grill at the proper height for the type of meat you are cooking and place the meat on top. To increase the smokiness, mist the charcoal with the sprayer and close the lid of the grill immediately.

You might also first soak hickory or other hardwood chips in water for 1 hour and add them to the coals when you build your fire, or make the whole fire from hardwood, which will give your meat a subtly smoky taste. Hickory, alder, oak, mesquite, and fruitwoods (orchard trees) are best.

HOME SMOKERS

Once you've tasted some of this great barbecue, you may decide to go even further to get that great down-home taste and purchase a smoker.

Smoking is a slow process. The meat cooks over very low heat in an enclosed space, smoke and moisture circulating around it to create that special succulence. With such a slow, gentle method, meat shrinks very little.

Smoking may or may not totally cook the meat, so you should make sure that whatever you are smoking reaches a safe internal temperature (pork especially). Generally you can smoke the meat long enough so that it needs no additional cooking in an oven. But if you are in doubt, a little extra heating won't hurt.

GAS OR ELECTRIC SMOKERS These are simple boxlike structures with a heating element in the bottom, a pan that fits on top of the heat and holds the smoldering chips or chunks of wood, and racks located above these to hold the item being smoked. They are thermostatically controlled, and are mini-versions of the kind of smokers used in barbecue restaurants.

If you buy a small electric smoker, save the box. It turns out to be the key to the whole smoking operation, especially in cold weather. The cardboard packing box should be left around the smoker when it's in use, acting as an insulator to keep the heat in.

CHARCOAL OR WOOD SMOKERS These smokers are rather small and look like a loaf cake pan sitting double-deck over another loaf cake pan. They are used the world around relying on hardwood chips, coals, or sawdust for their smoke. The advantage of these cookers is their simplicity. Their disadvantage is that they require careful watching. A smoky fire must be maintained and the heat, approximately 180°F (80°C), depending on the cut and type of meat you are smoking, must be kept even.

CHARCOAL WATER SMOKERS AND CHINESE SMOKERS The water smoker functions much like standard charcoal smokers, with the addition of a pan of liquid (water and marinade) placed between the charcoal and the grill so that the meat in effect self-bastes during the smoking process, adding to its juiciness. (They also come in electric versions.)

CHINESE SMOKERS, whether permanent brick or movable metal, are always L-shaped, with an upright chimney. The meat hangs from hooks in the chimney, away from the coals, and the food is cooked in the hot smoke.

DO-IT-YOURSELF EQUIPMENT I've seen dozens of ingenious homemade smokers—using mailboxes, garbage cans, refrigerators—many of them as efficient as store-bought ones. They all work on the same basic principles: heating element in the bottom (an old hot plate, for instance), something to hold the wood chips (a cast-iron frying pan), a rack for the food (a discarded canning rack perhaps), and ventilation. There's no stopping the determined smoking enthusiast!

Wood

Store-bought smokers come supplied with a starter package of wood chips. If you use larger chunks of wood you won't need to check the smoker as frequently. Or you can use a mixture of the chips and larger chunks of wood. A combination of one-third each of packaged chips, chunks, and water works quite well. And, I might add, a little wood goes a long way. The wood should be soaked in water, kept wet, and replenished throughout the smoking process.

Use only hardwoods. Softwoods such as pine are not used for smoking because the resins give the meat an unpleasant taste. I found that hickory works best for beef and pork and that applewood gives poultry a wonderful flavor. You can usually purchase wood chips and chunks from the makers of the smokers.

TOOLS

Here, too, a few essential items do the trick. Some of them are just long-handled versions of familiar kitchen implements designed to keep you away from the hot coals.

TONGS Two pairs with long handles, one for food and one for coals. (Always turn meat with tongs to avoid puncturing it and losing precious juices.)

METAL SPATULA Long-handled, for turning food.

FORK Long-handled, for prodding and pulling vegetables, never meat.

BASTING BRUSH Long-handled, for brushing sauce onto the meat during the cooking process.

HINGED WIRE GRILL BASKET For foods that require frequent turning such as burgers, chops, and shrimp.

OVEN MITTS For adjusting the rack and turning the basket.

MEAT THERMOMETER For larger cuts, because you may think the meat is done when it isn't.

PLANT MISTER OR PUMP SPRAY BOTTLE FILLED WITH WATER To douse flare-ups.

SAUCES

Sauces add considerably to the difference in flavor from one barbecue to another. Each part of the country has its own favorite, and I've tested and tasted for years to determine the very best of these.

Sauces vary greatly. There are sweet ketchup-base Middle South ones; tart mustard or vinegar types from the Carolinas; garlicky, spicy-hot Southwestern versions; plus fruity ones and Asian-inspired soy-ginger-garlic sauces from the West Coast. And of course there are shades of everything else in between. Personally, I've always preferred thick, red, strongly spiced, sweet-sour, smoky, garlicky sauces with a pungent flavor balance, using the freshest and purest ingredients.

Whatever your preference, the sauces included in this book are the *best* from all over the United States that you can use to make home-cooked, finger-lickin' barbecue. These sauces can be used over meats, poultry, and fish cooked in your oven broiler or outside on the grill. I usually choose indoor barbecuing for the sauces with a high sugar content since the sauce tends to blacken less when cooked indoors.

I've suggested my favorite pairings of sauces and meats or fish—but don't limit yourself. Be creative and you'll discover even more gorgeous combinations! (The sauces can be used when you're smoking meats too. Follow the manufacturer's instructions for smoking, then add the sauce and dig in.) Barbecue sauce improves nearly every food it gets put on!

SAUCE NOTES

- Most of the recipes that follow make enough sauce for you to have extra at the table—and also leave you some to freeze. I've listed the maximum amount of meat the sauce will cover in each recipe, but of course you can cook less and save the additional sauce for another meal.

- Allow 1/3 to 1/2 cup of sauce per pound of meat.

- Leave the pot uncovered when you're cooking the sauce so it will reduce to its desired consistency.

- The amount of salt given in the recipes is only a guide. You may want to wait and add salt to taste after the sauce has finished cooking—a great many sauce ingredients contain substantial amounts of salt and when reduced become even saltier.

- As a rule, do not start basting meat with a ketchup- or tomato-based sauce until the meat is one-third done, as the sugar and sweeteners in the ingredients have a tendency to burn quickly over high heat.

- All sauces can be prepared ahead and stored in the refrigerator for up to a week—or keep them in the freezer for as long as three months. They'll make an ordinary meat dish special.

- To eliminate loss of sauce, to prevent sauce from burning, and to facilitate cleanup, cover the grill with heavy-duty aluminum foil and punch holes in the foil with a knife to allow for ventilation. But sear the meat first on both sides before placing it on the foil. This will seal in the smoky taste.

- Serve leftover sauce along with the cooked meat.

- When storing in the refrigerator, do not use foil to cover meats cooked with an acid-based sauce (tomato or lemon, for example) because the sauce will eat holes in the foil, which will taint the flavor of the sauce and the meat.

- If you marinated meat in the sauce, wipe the sauce off with a paper towel before searing the meat so it will brown well.

MARINADE

A marinade is an aromatic blend of herbs and vegetables in which meat, poultry, or fish can be soaked so it will absorb the flavors and become more tender. Usually the ingredients include oil to lubricate the flesh and an additional liquid, most often an acid (wine, vinegar, or fruit juice), which serves to tenderize the meat. A baste, on the other hand, is a liquid that is applied to the food as it cooks, giving a flavor to the surface.

COOKING MEATS

- If meat is to be cooked without sauce, oil the grill with 1 to 2 Tablespoons of vegetable or olive oil to prevent the meat from sticking to it. Or you may grease it with the fat trimmed from the meat to be cooked.
- Cook pork slowly and thoroughly: for fresh pork, 20 to 25 minutes per inch of thickness; for smoked pork, 15 to 20 minutes per inch of thickness.
- Meat will cook faster if brought to room temperature (70°F, 20°C) in advance. This takes about 20 to 30 minutes in a warm kitchen and up to 1 hour in a cooler room, depending on the cut and size of the meat.
- Trim cuts of meat of all excess fat before grilling, leaving 1/4 inch around the edges.
- Cuts of beef and lamb for outdoor grilling should be a minimum of 1 1/2 inches thick, but not more than 3 inches thick, to remain pink inside after the surface sears. Pork should always be at least 1 inch thick, but never thicker than 1/2 inches because thorough cooking is necessary.
- Ribs will be juicier if they are cooked in large pieces (racks). If cut into serving pieces, they'll be crisp and more surfaces will be glazed with the sauce.
- In true barbecue, the meat is never touched by the flame.

Barbecue sauces ordinarily are brushed onto the food as it cooks, as a baste. However, since they contain many of the same ingredients, they can function as a marinade also.

For small cuts allow 1 hour per inch of thickness, at room temperature; and 3 hours per inch of thickness when refrigerated. For larger cuts of meat allow 4 to 6 hours at room temperature, or from 1 to 2 days in the refrigerator, depending on the size of the cut. Turn the meat occasionally to distribute the marinade. Just remember to wipe off any extra sauce before you sear the meat in order for it to brown well.

Always marinate in a noncorrosive container such as glass, porcelain, glazed earthenware, or stainless steel. Leave the dish uncovered to allow air to circulate.

LIQUID SMOKE

Basically, the easiest way to gain a smoky taste in any barbecue or curing process is to carefully apply liquid smoke. Made by burning damp hickory wood, condensing the smoke, and scientifically processing it to remove the tars and resins, the US Department of Agriculture considers liquid smoke a natural food product. It contains no calories and has been accepted as a "legal" product for dieters. It contains less than 1 milligram of sodium per tablespoon.

Liquid smoke seems to have originated in Kansas City and was first marketed in 1895 in Ulysses, Nebraska, by one family, the Wrights. It was an immediate success because it replaced time-consuming smokehouse techniques with an easy-to-use liquid. Once the meat was cured, the smoky taste could be brushed on or added drop by drop, saving much energy.

Wright's Liquid Smoke is still in business and has relocated to Tennessee. The bottles are much fancier nowadays; they've even come up with a spray bottle so you don't have to pour it onto the meat. When I was a kid, you had to let the liquid smoke drip very carefully. We always used a soft cloth to dab it sparingly on the meat, and even then only used it when time and circumstance prevented enjoying and taking part in the real thing.

Using this product is really a matter of personal preference. It works well and tastes great when used in the proper proportions. Because of its concentrated nature, liquid smoke should be added with discretion to sauces. I still feel that nothing really substitutes for the real smoke.

ROASTING TEMPERATURES

(Place meat thermometer in the center, not touching the bone.)

Beef	Rare: 140°F (60°C)
	Medium: 160°F (70°C)
	Well done: 170°F (75°C)
Pork	170°F (75°C)
Chicken	Breast: 170°F (75°C)
	Thigh: 180°F (80°C)
Duck	Thigh: 170°F (75°C)
Turkey	Breast: 170°F (75°C)
	Thigh: 180°F (80°C)
Lamb	Rare: 140°F (60°C)
	Medium: 160°F (70°C)
	Well done: 170°–180°F (75°C–80°C)

Outdoor Barbecue

Barbecuing on your outdoor grill, when you follow these recipes, results in finger lickin', sumptuously sauced meats, not just simple steaks or chops. These very finest of sauce recipes from all over the USA, coupled with hearty ribs and chops, chicken and seafood, should tempt you to dust off your grill and allow yourself to experience the passionate delights of authentic, honest-to-goodness, old-fashioned barbecue.

Jane's Best Barbecued Ribs

I have been developing this sauce for several years, and now it's a real winner and my all-time Southwestern favorite. It's particularly great served over lean baby back pork ribs, but you can also serve it on chicken. Ears of corn grilled in the husk, freshly baked cornbread, and homemade coleslaw served alongside make a fabulous feast.

    2 Tablespoons bacon drippings
    1 medium Spanish onion, finely chopped
    1 clove garlic, minced
    1 (14-ounce) bottle ketchup
    6 Tablespoons Worcestershire sauce
    2 Tablespoons cider vinegar
    1/4 cup dry white wine
    1 teaspoon dry mustard
    2 Tablespoons firmly packed dark brown sugar
    1 to 2 Tablespoons pure ground hot red chile or to taste
    1 to 2 Tablespoons pure ground mild red chile or to taste
    1/4 teaspoon cayenne pepper or pequin quebrado (preferable)
    3/4 teaspoon ground cumin
    1/4 teaspoon ground coriander seed
    1 teaspoon liquid smoke
    4 to 6 pounds baby back pork ribs, in uncut racks

TO PREPARE THE SAUCE

Melt the bacon drippings in a 2-quart saucepan over medium heat, then add the onion and garlic, and sauté until the onion is transparent. Add the ketchup, Worcestershire, cider vinegar, wine, mustard, brown sugar, hot red chile, mild red chile, cayenne pepper, cumin, coriander, and liquid smoke, reduce the heat to low, and simmer, uncovered, for 15 minutes, stirring occasionally. Set the sauce aside until you are ready to use it.

Makes 3 cups.

TO BARBECUE THE RIBS

When the fire is ready, position the rack 3 inches above the heat source. Place the racks of ribs on the grill and sear the meat for 2 minutes per side. Remove the meat from the grill, raise the rack 2 inches, and cover it with a layer of heavy-duty broiler foil. Puncture the foil to make plenty of ventilation holes. Place the ribs on the foil and generously spoon on the barbecue sauce. Allow the ribs to cook for 15 minutes before turning them and saucing the second side.

Once the second side is basted, cook the ribs for an additional 15 minutes before turning and saucing them again. Allow the ribs to grill for 10 minutes. Then turn and sauce them one final time. After 10 more minutes, both sides of the ribs should have a crisp glaze. Continue saucing and turning until a sharp knife inserted between the ribs shows no pink meat.

Transfer the racks to a carving board, cut the ribs apart, and pile them on platters for guests to help themselves.

Makes 4 to 6 servings.

James Beal's Barbecued Ribs

In the spring of 1981, John Hinterberger of the *Seattle* Times discovered that town's J. K. Wild Boar Soul BBQ Pit and its affable owner, James Beal, a Dallas native. In his laudatory review of Beal's great barbecue, Hinterberger said that according to Beal, what really makes barbecue work is long, slow cooking, preferably in a smoke chamber indirectly heated by the fire source. (The ribs at the Wild Boar cook a minimum of 14 hours at very low temperatures. Folks have been known to faint with anticipation.)

Beal seasons the meat only slightly during cooking, dusting it with a mixture of seasoned salt and paprika. The barbecue sauce goes on afterward; otherwise, the sugar would turn the ribs black during the cooking process. The meat receives its final glaze of gorgeous goop when it is served. You need to spend as much time fussing with the sauce as you do with the meat.

3/4 cup white sugar
1/2 cup firmly packed dark brown sugar
2/3 cup rich, dark beef base made from double-strength beef bouillon or consommé
1 quart hot water
2/3 cup prepared yellow mustard
1/3 cup white vinegar
1/3 cup liquid smoke
2/3 cup Worcestershire sauce
1 1/3 cups tomato paste
3 Tablespoons pure ground hot red chile or to taste
5 medium-size marinated jalapeño peppers, finely diced
12 pounds baby back ribs, in uncut racks
2 teaspoons seasoned salt
2 teaspoons paprika

To Prepare the Sauce

In a 3-quart saucepan, mix the white sugar, brown sugar, and beef base in the water. Cook over medium heat until the mixture is dissolved. Add the mustard, vinegar, liquid smoke, Worcestershire, tomato paste, ground chile, and jalapeños and simmer, uncovered, over low heat for 2 hours. Set aside until you are ready to barbecue.

Makes 1 1/2 quarts.

To Barbecue the Ribs

When the fire is ready, position the rack 3 inches above the heat source. Sprinkle the ribs on both sides with the seasoned salt and the paprika. Place the racks of ribs on the grill and sear the meat for 2 minutes per side. When the meat is seared, raise the rack 2 inches. Allow the ribs to cook for 15 minutes before turning them.

Once the second side has cooked, turn the ribs and cook them for an additional 15 minutes before turning them again. Allow the ribs to grill for 10 minutes more, then turn them one final time. After another 10 minutes both sides of the ribs should have a crisp glaze. The ribs will be done when a sharp knife inserted between the ribs shows no pink meat.

Transfer the racks to a carving board, cut the ribs apart, and pile them on platters for guests to serve themselves, accompanied, of course, by some of James Beal's fabulous sauce.

Makes 10 to 12 servings.

Super-Secret Baby Back Pork Ribs

A retired cook shared this secret with me because I promised not to reveal the name of the restaurant that made these ribs famous. When cooked in their original setting, the ribs were specially smoked, but this backyard version is just as irresistibly delicious. Serve them with crusty hollows of sourdough garlic bread.*

1 Tablespoon Worcestershire sauce
1/2 cup cider vinegar
2 cups tomato sauce
1/2 cup firmly packed dark brown sugar
1 large clove garlic, finely minced
1/4 teaspoon celery salt
Pinch of allspice
1 Tablespoon freshly grated onion
2 Tablespoons pure ground hot red chile
1/4 teaspoon cayenne pepper or pequin quebrado (preferable)
4 pounds baby back pork ribs, in uncut racks

TO PREPARE THE SAUCE

In a 2-quart saucepan combine the Worcestershire, cider vinegar, tomato sauce, brown sugar, garlic, celery salt, allspice, onion, ground chile, and cayenne pepper and simmer, uncovered, over low heat until the sauce is thickened. Set the sauce aside until you are ready to use it.

Makes 3 cups.

Note: This barbecue sauce also works well as a marinade.

TO BARBECUE THE RIBS

About 2 to 4 hours before you are planning to cook the meat, place the racks of ribs in a roasting pan large enough to hold them in a single layer or divide the meat between two pans. To marinate use only 1/2 to 2/3 of the sauce and spoon it over the meat, making sure both sides are well covered. Of the remaining sauce, set aside half to serve with the cooked ribs. Reserve the rest to use as a baste during the cooking.

Let the marinating ribs sit, uncovered, and turn after each hour. Spoon sauce over the racks after each turn. Do not refrigerate the ribs during the marinating time as refrigeration slows down the meat's ability to absorb flavors.

When you are ready to cook the meat, remove the ribs from the marinade. Add the marinade to the sauce you reserved for basting. Position the grill rack 3 inches above the heat source. Place the racks of ribs on the grill and sear the meat for 5 minutes per side. Remove the meat from the grill, raise the rack another 2 inches, and cover it with a layer of heavy-duty broiler foil. Puncture the foil to make ventilation holes.

Place the ribs on the foil and generously spoon on the reserved basting sauce. Allow the ribs to cook for 15 minutes before turning them and saucing the second side. Once the second side is basted, cook the ribs for an additional 15 minutes before turning and saucing again. Allow the ribs to grill for 10 minutes, then turn and sauce them one final time. After 10 more minutes, both sides of the ribs should have a crisp glaze.

Transfer the racks to a carving board, cut the ribs apart into easy-to-serve portions, and pile them on platters for guests to help themselves. Serve with the sauce specifically set aside for table use.

Makes 4 servings.

*To prepare a foot-long loaf of garlic bread, melt 4 Tablespoons unsalted butter with 1/4 cup olive oil in a small sauce pan over low heat, then add freshly minced garlic to taste. Raise the heat and brown the garlic for a few seconds. Halve the bread lengthwise, brush the butter and garlic mixture on each half, and toast them in the oven or over the grill.

Fiery Hot and South Carolina Pork

These recipes come from David Brown, owner of the famous Hickory House Pit BBQ in Winnsboro, South Carolina. He has a strong preference for these sauces because they don't hide the pork flavor as ketchup- or mustard-base sauces have a tendency to do. Both sauces are too strong to be used as a marinade and neither needs to be cooked before using it to baste the pork. The meat should be cooked in a kettle or wagon-type grill (see page 5), and the cooking instructions that follow are good for both sauce recipes.

FIERY HOT BASTING SAUCE

2 cups cider vinegar
1 Tablespoon Worcestershire sauce
1 Tablespoon finely ground black pepper
1 Tablespoon liquid hot pepper sauce
1/2 Tablespoon salt or to taste
2 pounds pork butt or shoulder

In a bowl combine the cider vinegar, Worcestershire, black pepper, hot pepper sauce, and salt and mix well. Add the pork butt or shoulder. Allow the flavors to mellow for at least 1 hour at room temperature.

Makes 2 cups.

SOUTH CAROLINA BASTING SAUCE

2 cups cider vinegar
1 Tablespoon freshly ground black pepper
1 Tablespoon cayenne pepper
1 Tablespoon vegetable oil
2 pounds pork butt or shoulder

Combine the cider vinegar, black pepper, cayenne pepper, and vegetable oil in a bowl and mix well. Add the pork butt or shoulder. Allow the flavors to mellow for at least 1 hour at room temperature.

Makes 2 cups.

TO BARBECUE THE PORK

When the fire is ready, position the rack 5 inches above the heat source. Place the meat on the grill and sear it for 2 minutes per side. When the meat is seared, baste it with either sauce and close the lid on the grill. After 15 minutes turn the meat and baste again, then close the lid. Continue turning and basting every 15 minutes until the meat falls from the bone, about 1 to 1 1/2 hours. Transfer the meat to a cutting board, cut it into bite-size pieces, and serve.

Makes 4 servings.

"BBCs" (Beer Barbecued Pork Chops)

Bill Zubke, 1979 winner of the South Dakota Pork Cookout, developed this winning recipe using a well-seasoned brew that he serves on pork loin chops.

1/4 cup cider vinegar
1/4 cup Worcestershire sauce
1/4 cup (1/2 stick) unsalted butter
1 medium onion, chopped
1 Tablespoon celery seed
2 cloves fresh garlic, finely minced
1 teaspoon dry mustard
1 teaspoon sugar
1 teaspoon salt
1 teaspoon cayenne pepper or freshly ground black pepper
1 (14-ounce) bottle ketchup
1 cup flat beer (fresh beer will work too)
8 loin pork chops, 1 to 1/4 inches thick

TO PREPARE THE SAUCE

In a 2-quart saucepan combine the cider vinegar, Worcestershire, butter, onion, celery seed, garlic, mustard, sugar, salt, pepper, ketchup, and beer. Simmer, uncovered, over medium heat for 15 minutes. Stir frequently to blend the flavors. Set the sauce aside until you are ready to barbecue.

Makes 3 cups.

TO BARBECUE THE PORK

When the fire is ready, position the rack 3 inches above the heat source. Place the chops on the rack and sear the meat for 5 minutes on each side. Remove the chops from the grill. Raise the rack another 2 inches, and cover it with a layer of heavy-duty broiler foil. Poke ventilation holes in the foil.

Return the chops to the grill and generously spoon on the sauce. Cook for 10 minutes, then turn the meat and generously sauce the second side. Continue turning and saucing the chops every 5 minutes until they are cooked through, a total of 30 to 40 minutes. To test for doneness, cut through to the bone of a chop. If the meat is white, with no pink showing, the chop is done.

Makes 4 servings.

Hamburgers Made Special

Use leftover barbecue sauce to make hamburgers something special. Don't add the sauce to the raw meat. First sear the burger on one side, then turn it and sauce the cooked side. When the second side is seared, turn the burger again and sauce the second side. Continue to cook and sauce the hamburger until it's done to your taste.

These sauces taste especially good on burgers:
- Jane's Best (page 14)
- James Beal's (page 15)
- Super-Secret (page 16)
- Outrageous (page 30)
- Down Home Louisiana (page 31)
- Jerry's Beef (page 42)
- San Francisco (page 50)

New Mexico Barbecued Beef Ribs

Served northern New Mexico–style, short ribs would be accompanied by stewed pinto beans, more of the red chile sauce, green chile relish (see note), and steaming homemade wheat tortillas. A simple vegetable salad and lots of cold Mexican beer followed by Mexican coffee, tart, chilled fresh fruits, and crisp, sweet, spicy cookies (New Mexican anise-flavored biscochitos, if possible) for dessert complete this feast with minimal work.

1/3 cup Red Chile Sauce (recipe follows)
1 cup dry red wine
2 Tablespoons olive oil
1 large clove garlic, minced
1 small Spanish onion, diced
1/2 teaspoon salt
1/4 teaspoon freshly ground black pepper
4 pounds beef short ribs

To Prepare the Sauce

The night before your barbecue, prepare the Red Chile Sauce.

Two hours before your barbecue, combine the 1/3 cup Red Chile Sauce, red wine, olive oil, garlic, onion, salt, and black pepper. Allow the marinade to sit at room temperature for 15 minutes to blend flavors.

Makes 1 2/3 cups.

To Barbecue the Ribs

Spread the ribs out in a roasting pan large enough to hold them in a single layer. Pour the sauce over the ribs, making sure each one is well covered. Turn and rub the ribs with sauce several times. It is not necessary to refrigerate the ribs.

When the fire is ready, position the rack 3 inches above the heat source. Remove the ribs from the marinade and reserve the marinade in a bowl or pitcher to use for basting. Place the ribs on the grill and sear for 10 minutes on each side. Remove the ribs from the grill, raise the rack another 2 inches above the heat source, and cover it with a layer of heavy-duty broiler foil. Poke ventilation holes in the foil. Return the ribs to the grill and spoon on the reserved marinade. Cook for 5 minutes, then turn and baste the second side.

Continue turning and basting every 5 minutes until the ribs are done, 30 to 40 minutes. The meat should be slightly pink inside and crusty brown outside.

Makes 4 servings.

Note: Prepare green chile relish by roasting green chiles alongside the ribs until charred. While the meat continues to cook, quickly chill (a freezer will do it quickly), peel, and dice the chiles. Add freshly minced garlic and salt, and your relish is ready.

RED CHILE SAUCE

You will need only 1/3 cup of this sauce for the barbecue marinade. The additional sauce should be served at the table.

2 Tablespoons bacon drippings or lard
2 Tablespoons all-purpose flour
1/4 cup pure ground mild red chile or to taste
2 cups beef bouillon or water
1 clove garlic, finely minced
3/4 teaspoon salt or to taste
1/4 teaspoon ground oregano (Mexican oregano, if you can get it)
1/4 teaspoon ground cumin

In a 2-quart saucepan melt the drippings or lard over medium heat. Slowly add the flour, stirring to combine thoroughly, and cook the mixture until it turns golden. Remove the pan from the heat and stir in the ground chile. When it is well incorporated, add the bouillon, stir, and return the pan to the heat. Add the garlic, salt, oregano, and cumin and simmer, uncovered, for 30 minutes or longer to develop the flavor. Taste, and adjust the seasonings if necessary. Allow the sauce to cool, then transfer it to an airtight container and refrigerate.

Makes 2 cups.

—— Terry Johnson's Hawaiian Luau Barbecued Beef Ribs ——

Hailing from Hawaii and the winner of the Nevada State Chili Contest in 1980, Terry has another passion . . . barbecue! She uses this marinade with meaty beef short ribs and the raves don't stop. Serve them Hawaiian-style surrounded by flowers and orange wedges or pineapple slices. Accompany the ribs with rice molds (see note). A fresh fruit salad tops off this perfect barbecue.

1 cup soy sauce
6 Tablespoons firmly packed dark brown sugar
1 cup water
2/3 cup dry sherry
2 teaspoons pure ground hot red chile or to taste
2 teaspoons Chinese Five Spice powder*
3 teaspoons minced fresh ginger
2 teaspoons minced garlic
4 to 6 pounds beef short ribs

To Prepare the Sauce

In a small saucepan combine soy sauce, brown sugar, water, sherry, ground chile, Chinese Five Spice powder, ginger, and garlic. Cook over medium heat to dissolve the sugar, but do *not* boil. Remove the marinade from the heat and let it cool. Set it aside until you are ready to marinate the ribs.

Makes 2 1/2 cups.

*Chinese Five Spice powder is available at Chinese specialty stores and in the gourmet food section of some supermarkets.

To Barbecue the Ribs

Two hours before your barbecue, spread the ribs out in a roasting pan large enough to hold them in a single layer or divide the meat between two pans. Pour the sauce over the ribs, making sure all the meat is well covered. Turn and rub the ribs with the sauce several times during the marinating period. It is not necessary to refrigerate the ribs.

When the fire is ready, position the rack 3 inches above the heat source. Remove the ribs from the marinade and reserve the marinade in a bowl or pitcher, including any excess scraped off the ribs, for basting. Place the ribs on the grill and sear for 10 minutes each side. Spoon on the reserved marinade a little at a time after each turn. Cook for 5 minutes, then turn and baste the second side. Continue turning and basting every 5 minutes until the ribs are done, 30 to 40 minutes. The meat should be slightly pink on the inside and crusty brown on the outside.

Makes 4 to 6 servings.

Note: Make rice molds by simply pressing cooked rice into 1/3-cup-size buttered ramekins, then steaming them in an inch of water for about 10 minutes before unmolding and serving. You could also reserve some of the sauce before marinating the meet and add to the unmolded cooked rice plus 2 Tablespoons each of chopped Bermuda onion and slivered toasted almonds. Garnish each portion of rice with minced parsley after you unmold it.

Alabama Smoky Barbecued Chicken

This recipe (dedicated to Harold Newman of Waverly, Alabama) comes to me courtesy of Pfaffman Studios, Brooklyn, New York, where my friends Scott Pfaffman and Florence Neil have the most fabulous outdoor barbecues on the roof of their loft. Their chicken is cooked in homemade barrel smokers, but you can get the same effect with any covered grill. It's some of the best barbecued chicken I've come across in quite a while.

    4 cups tomato sauce
    1/2 cup light soy sauce
    1/2 cup white vinegar
    12 ounces flat beer (fresh beer will work too)
    1 Tablespoon salt
    1 Tablespoon pure ground hot red chile
    1 Tablespoon freshly ground black pepper
    3 large cloves garlic, finely minced
    8 (3- to 4-pound) chickens, quartered or cut into serving pieces

Preheat the oven to 450°F (230°C). In a 2-quart saucepan combine the tomato sauce, soy sauce, vinegar, beer, salt, ground chile, black pepper, and garlic and allow the sauce to simmer, uncovered, over low heat for 20 minutes. Stir to combine well.

Meanwhile, place the chicken pieces in large oiled baking pans skin side up and bake for 45 minutes in the preheated oven. Remove the chicken from the oven. Pour off the collected pan juices and fat, reserving 1 cup. Add this cup to the sauce on the stove. Bring the sauce to a boil, then lower the heat and simmer for 15 minutes. Pour the sauce over the chicken (still in the pans) and marinate the chicken in it for 1 hour at room temperature, basting frequently with the sauce.

In the meantime, start the fire in your grill, using wood scraps (not charcoal lighter). When the fire is ready, cover the rack with a layer of heavy-duty broiler foil (puncture it with plenty of holes for ventilation) and position it 5 inches above the heat source. Remove the chicken from the marinade. Pour the marinade into a bowl to use to baste the chicken as it grills. Place the chicken on the rack, skin side up, and cover the grill with its lid (or with a foil tent; puncture plenty of holes for ventilation). You want the chicken to cook slowly.

Baste the chicken with the sauce frequently, then turn the pieces after 30 minutes. Keep the fire under control by occasionally spraying it with water from a spray bottle. Continue cooking the chicken, basting often, for 60 to 70 minutes, or until it is very tender and smoky. When the chicken is cooked, remove it from the grill and serve it with the remaining sauce.

Makes 12 to 15 servings.

To Make a Foil Tent (*FOR A GRILL WITH NO COVER*)

To create this pyramid-shape lid for your grill you need two 4-x-4-foot lengths of 18-inch-wide, heavy-duty broiler foil. Lay one sheet of foil on top of the other, dull side out. Fold together one long edge, making first a 1/4-inch fold, then a second 1/4-inch fold. Open up the foil. You should have one big sheet securely fastened down the center.

Halfway along each long and short side, make a deep tuck. The foil should peak in the center to make a pyramid-shape tent, shiny side in. To stabilize the tent, turn up an inch all along the bottom edge. Place the tent over your grill after the meat has been placed on the rack. Using the tent will add to the smoky flavor of the meat.

— Sunny Arizona's Special Chicken —

This spicy-hot sauce also tastes wonderful when added to a pulled pork butt. For instructions on how to pull meat see page 39.

4 pickled jalapeño peppers, stemmed, seeded, and finely minced
2 large cloves garlic, finely minced
1 teaspoon dry mustard
1 teaspoon dried sweet basil
1 teaspoon oregano, rubbed to a powder
2 teaspoons kosher salt
3 Tablespoons fresh orange juice
1/4 cup honey
3 Tablespoons red wine vinegar
2 Tablespoons vegetable oil
1 small onion, finely minced
3 cups crushed canned tomatoes
5 to 6 pounds chicken, cut into serving pieces

TO PREPARE THE SAUCE

Make sure the and garlic are very finely minced. In a ceramic bowl combine the minced jalapeños and garlic with the dry mustard, basil, oregano, salt, orange juice, honey, and red wine vinegar. Set aside.

In a 2-quart saucepan heat the oil over medium heat, then add the onion and sauté until softened but not browned. Stir in the tomatoes and add the jalapeño mixture. Bring the sauce to a boil. Reduce the heat and simmer, uncovered, stirring occasionally, for 40 minutes, or until it has been reduced to a desirable thickness. Taste and correct the seasonings.

Makes 3 cups.

TO BARBECUE THE CHICKEN

When the fire is ready, position the rack 5 inches above the heat source. Place the chicken pieces on the hot rack, skin side down. When seared, turn and grill the pieces bone side down, until light golden. Remove the chicken from the grill and cover the rack with a layer of heavy-duty broiler foil. Puncture the foil to make plenty of ventilation holes.

Place the chicken on the foil, skin side down, and generously spoon on the barbecue sauce. Grill until the sauce is set. Then turn the pieces over, sauce the skin side, and grill bone side down. Continue saucing and turning until all the pieces are done, about 50 to 60 minutes. To test for doneness, insert the tip of a sharp knife into the largest piece of chicken breast. If the juices run clear, it's done.

Makes 4 to 6 servings.

Jerry Wood's Personal Favorite Barbecued Chicken

North Carolina native Jerry Wood is president of Brookwood Farms, a very successful manufacturer of barbecued pork for commercial distribution. Obviously an avid barbecue enthusiast, he shares this personal favorite for chicken barbecue. "With this recipe," Jerry says, "you can do no wrong!"

1 cup ketchup
1 cup cider vinegar
1 cup water
4 Tablespoons firmly packed light brown sugar
1/2 cup prepared yellow mustard
1/2 cup (1 stick) unsalted butter
2 teaspoons salt or to taste
1 teaspoon cayenne pepper
1/4 cup Worcestershire sauce
8 to 10 pounds chicken, cut into serving pieces

To Prepare the Sauce

In a 2-quart saucepan combine ketchup, cider vinegar, water, brown sugar, mustard, butter, salt, cayenne pepper, and Worcestershire and cook together, uncovered, until somewhat thickened, about 30 minutes. Set aside until you are ready to barbecue.

Makes 1 quart.

To Barbecue the Chicken

When the fire is ready, position the rack 5 inches above the heat source. Place the chicken pieces on the hot rack, skin side down. When seared, turn and grill the pieces bone side down, until light golden.

Remove the chicken from the grill and cover the grill with a layer of heavy-duty broiler foil. Puncture the foil to make plenty of ventilation holes. Place the chicken on the foil, skin side down, and generously spoon on the barbecue sauce. Grill until the sauce is set. Then turn the pieces over, sauce the skin side, and grill bone side down.

Continue saucing and turning until all the pieces are done, about 50 to 60 minutes. To test for doneness, insert the tip of a sharp knife into the largest piece of chicken breast. If the juices run clear, it's done.

Makes 8 to 10 servings.

Anthony's Sicilian Barbecued Chicken

This is a very special relish-type barbecue recipe that I discovered in a rather unusual way. En route to judge a chili contest, I struck up a conversation with the limousine driver, a retired New York policeman who loved to cook. When he found out that I also loved to cook and actually wrote cookbooks, he offered to share his all-time favorite recipe, which happens to be a very flavorful Italian-style chicken barbecue sauce that is also wonderful as a relish on cheese and crackers when you're in need of a creative snack. Anthony says he can never make enough of this sauce.

1 Tablespoon vegetable oil
1 medium onion, finely chopped
1/4 cup finely minced fresh parsley
1 clove garlic, finely minced
1/2 cup firmly packed dark brown sugar
1 cup water
3 to 4 large ripe tomatoes, peeled, seeded, and chopped or pureed, enough to measure 2 cups
1/2 fresh lemon, juiced
1/2 fresh orange, juiced
1 teaspoon red wine vinegar
1 Tablespoon paprika
1 teaspoon salt or to taste
1/4 teaspoon freshly ground black pepper
6 pounds chicken, cut into serving pieces

To Prepare the Sauce

In a heavy saucepan heat the oil over medium heat. Add the onion, parsley, and garlic and sauté until the onions are golden.

In the meantime, dissolve the brown sugar in the water. Add this sugar-water mixture and the tomatoes to the onion mixture in the saucepan and cook, uncovered, until thickened, about 30 minutes. Add the tomatoes, lemon juice, orange juice, red wine vinegar, paprika, salt, and black pepper and cook until the sauce has thickened to the consistency of jam. Set aside until you are ready to barbecue.

Makes 3 1/2 cups.

To Barbecue the Chicken

When the fire is ready, position the rack 5 inches above the heat source. Place the chicken pieces on the hot rack, skin side down. When seared, turn and grill the pieces bone side down, until light golden. Remove the chicken from the grill and cover the grill with a layer of heavy-duty broiler foil. Puncture the foil to make plenty of ventilation holes.

Place the chicken on the foil, skin side down, and generously spoon on the barbecue sauce. Grill until the sauce is set. Then turn the pieces over, sauce the skin side, and grill bone side down. Continue saucing and turning until all the pieces are done, about 50 to 60 minutes. To test for doneness, insert the tip of a sharp knife into the largest piece of chicken breast. If the juices run clear, it's done.

Makes 4 to 6 servings.

Southwest Chicken BBQ

An easy-to-do hot, spicy barbecue sauce to use when time is short. It's great on pork or beef ribs too.

  1 cup ketchup
  5 Tablespoons unsalted butter, or use salted butter and omit the salt listed below
  1/4 cup strong black coffee
  3 Tablespoons Worcestershire sauce
  1 to 2 Tablespoons pure ground hot red chile or chile caribe (crushed red chile)
  1 Tablespoon firmly packed dark brown sugar
  1/4 teaspoon salt or to taste
  3 to 4 pounds chicken, cut into serving pieces

To Prepare the Sauce

In a 2-quart saucepan combine the ketchup, butter, coffee, Worcestershire, ground chile, brown sugar, and salt and allow the sauce to simmer, uncovered, over medium heat for 10 to 15 minutes. Set aside until you are ready to barbecue.

Makes 1 1/2 cups.

To Barbecue the Chicken

When the fire is ready, position the rack 5 inches above the heat source. Place the chicken pieces on the hot rack, skin side down. When seared, turn and grill the pieces bone side down, until light golden. Remove the chicken from the grill and cover the grill with a layer of heavy-duty broiler foil. Puncture the foil to make plenty of ventilation holes.

Place the chicken on the foil, skin side down, and generously spoon on the barbecue sauce. Grill until the sauce is set. Then turn the pieces over, sauce the skin side, and grill bone side down. Continue saucing and turning until all the pieces are done, about 50 to 60 minutes. To test for doneness, insert the tip of a sharp knife into the largest piece of chicken breast. If the juices run clear, it's done.

Makes 3 to 4 servings.

Outrageous Ham Steak

One steamy hot night in Georgia, I was privileged to sample the recipe of one of my favorite friends, professional cook Nathalie Dupree, who managed the cooking schools at Rich's Department Stores in Atlanta.

3/4 cup ketchup
1/4 cup cider vinegar
2 teaspoons Worcestershire sauce
1/4 teaspoon hot pepper sauce or to taste
2 Tablespoons prepared yellow mustard
1/4 cup molasses or firmly packed dark brown sugar
1/2 teaspoon salt
2 center-cut fully cooked ham steaks, 1 inch thick

TO PREPARE THE SAUCE

Combine ketchup, cider vinegar, Worcestershire, hot pepper sauce, mustard, molasses or brown sugar, and salt in a 2-quart saucepan and simmer, uncovered, over medium heat for 15 minutes. Set aside until you are ready to barbecue.

Makes 1 1/4 cups.

TO BARBECUE THE HAM

To rid the ham of excess salt and fat, first place the steaks in a large skillet in water to cover. Parboil them over medium-high heat for about 5 minutes. Pour off the water. Remove the steaks from the skillet and pat them dry with a paper towel. (This step is necessary *only* if you use country ham.)

Place the steaks in a large roasting pan and pour the sauce over them. Marinate the ham in the sauce for 20 minutes at room temperature. Remove the steaks from the pan, reserving the sauce. With a sharp knife, cut slashes in the fat around the edges of the steaks to prevent their curling during grilling.

When the fire is ready, grease the rack with a small piece of ham fat and position it 3 to 4 inches above the heat source. Place the ham steaks on the grill, and baste and turn frequently as they cook. The steaks will be done in 25 to 30 minutes.

Makes 4 servings.

Down Home Louisiana Barbecued Shrimp

I was given this recipe while visiting friends in Cajun country. They prepare the sauce one week in advance of the barbecue and then refrigerate it. I suggest you do the same—the flavors will have melded just the right amount during that time. Reheat the sauce when barbecue day arrives. Keep extra bowls of it on the table so guests who want more can serve themselves. Hush puppies (page 57), barbecued baked beans (page 55), and coleslaw (page 53) or a mixed green salad, and for dessert the Texas Pecan Cake (page 59) make for a super backyard party. In the South, gallons of sweetened iced tea and beer are served to quench the thirst.

2 cups ketchup
1 cup water
1/2 cup cider vinegar
3/4 cup sugar
2 cloves garlic, minced
1/2 cup finely chopped onion
1/2 cup finely diced green pepper
1/2 cup finely diced celery
1/4 cup finely minced fresh parsley
Juice and rind of 1 lemon
1/8 teaspoon liquid hot pepper sauce, or more to taste
1 1/2 Tablespoons Worcestershire sauce
1 1/2 teaspoons liquid smoke
1/2 teaspoon dried basil
1/2 teaspoon dried oregano
1/2 teaspoon ground cinnamon
1 Tablespoon bacon drippings
Salt to taste
5 pounds large shrimp, peeled and deveined

To Prepare the Sauce

In a 3-quart saucepan combine ketchup, water, cider vinegar, sugar, garlic, onion, green pepper, celery, parsley, juice and rind of lemon, hot pepper sauce, Worcestershire, liquid smoke, basil, oregano, cinnamon, and bacon drippings. Cook, uncovered, over medium heat, stirring frequently, until contents are reduced to 1 quart (4 cups), approximately 35 to 50 minutes. Taste and add salt if necessary. Allow the sauce to cool, then cover and refrigerate for 1 week before using.

Makes 1 quart.

To Barbecue the Shrimp

Allow the sauce to come to room temperature, then place it and the shrimp in a large bowl and marinate for 1 hour. Stir the shrimp in the sauce once or twice during the marinating period.

While the shrimp are marinating, prepare the grill. When the fire is ready, position the rack 4 inches above the heat source. Then cover it with a layer of heavy-duty broiler foil. Puncture the foil to make ventilation holes.

Place the shrimp in a hinged wire grill basket or spread the shrimp evenly on the prepared rack. Allow them to cook 1 minute, then brush them with the barbecue sauce and turn. Brush again with more sauce. Shrimp cook quickly and should be ready within 5 minutes.

Makes 4 to 6 servings.

Florida Shrimp

Way down south in sunny Florida, the orange influence shines, and for good reason. This sauce is as superb on chicken or ribs as it is on shrimp.

1/3 cup freshly squeezed lemon juice
1/3 cup freshly squeezed orange juice
1/3 cup chili sauce (ketchup-style)
1 clove garlic, minced
1 teaspoon dry mustard
1 Tablespoon Worcestershire sauce
1/4 cup honey
1/4 cup vegetable oil
1/4 teaspoon paprika
Salt and freshly ground black pepper to taste
1 1/2 pounds large shrimp, peeled and deveined

To Prepare the Sauce

Combine lemon juice, orange juice, chili sauce, garlic, mustard, Worcestershire, honey, oil, paprika, salt, and black pepper in a blender and blend thoroughly. Set the sauce aside until you are ready to barbecue the shrimp.

Makes 1 1/2 cups.

To Barbecue the Shrimp

When you are ready to barbecue, place the sauce and the shrimp in a large bowl and marinate for 1 hour. Stir the shrimp in the sauce once or twice during the marinating period.

While the shrimp are marinating, prepare the grill. When the fire is ready, position the rack 4 inches above the heat source, then cover it with a layer of heavy-duty broiler foil. Puncture the foil to make ventilation holes.

Place the shrimp in a hinged wire grill basket or spread the shrimp evenly on the prepared rack. Allow them to cook 1 minute, then brush them with the barbecue sauce and turn. Brush again with more sauce. Shrimp cook quickly and should be ready within 5 minutes.

Makes 2 to 3 servings.

INDOOR BARBECUE

No matter the time, the season, or the circumstance, you can savor the saucy goodness of succulent barbecues. Don't let bad weather or the absence of a grill, backyard, or patio keep you from this mouthwatering enjoyment. You can still approximate the flavor of barbecue in your oven.

The following recipes were chosen for this section because they work particularly well indoors, but most can be prepared outdoors. If you wish to try any of the recipes in the outdoor section in your oven broiler, go ahead. Just be sure not to baste the meat with the barbecue sauce until the final few minutes of cooking. Otherwise you will wind up with a crispy outside long before the inside of the meat is cooked.

Barbecued Pork

This recipe is great when you are hankering for that barbecue taste but time won't allow for long, slow cooking.

    1 pound coarsely ground pork
    2 teaspoons minced garlic
    1 medium onion, finely chopped
    1 cup sauce from Jane's Best Barbecued Ribs (recipe on page 14) or your favorite
    6 whole-wheat hamburger buns, split, lightly buttered, and toasted

In a bowl mix the pork with the garlic and onion. In a heavy skillet crumble the pork mixture and sauté over medium heat until the pork is thoroughly cooked. Drain well on paper towel–lined plate.

Return the pork to the skillet and add the barbecue sauce. Stir to combine well, then simmer gently over medium heat for 15 minutes. Place the split, toasted buns on serving plates, and let each person spoon on the barbecued pork.

Makes 2 to 3 servings.

Bernie's Asian Ribs

I savored these uniquely flavorful ribs one night quite by surprise. That day I had just completed a radio interview. Before the interview, I mentioned I was heading for the Catskills for relaxation and the announcer replied, "On the way, you really must try Bernie's Restaurant." He said that he knew I'd love it, and I did!

1/2 cup hoisin sauce,* or more to taste
1/2 cup mashed black bean sauce,* or more to taste
1 Tablespoon Sang Chow sauce* (optional)
18 ounces tomato puree
1 1/2 teaspoons ground ginger
1 1/2 teaspoons Chinese Five Spice powder*
1 1/2 teaspoons ground anise
10 ounces (5/8 cup) sugar
2 Tablespoons pureed fresh garlic
1 Tablespoon Tomato Shade*
3 Tablespoons salt, more or less, to taste
1 Tablespoon dry sherry
6 pounds baby back pork ribs

TO PREPARE THE SAUCE

In a bowl combine hoisin sauce, black bean sauce, Sang Chow sauce, tomato puree, ginger, Chinese Five Spice powder, anise, sugar, garlic, Tomato Shade, salt, and dry sherry, and mix together thoroughly.

*These items can be purchased at Asian food markets. Tomato Shade is the coloring traditionally used by Chinese cooks to give ribs their characteristic color. It adds no flavor, so don't worry if you can't find it locally.

TO BARBECUE THE RIBS

Preheat the oven to 400°F (205°C). Cut the ribs into serving-size pieces and place them in a glass dish. Spread the sauce on the ribs and let them sit for 4 to 6 hours at room temperature, or covered overnight in the refrigerator if you prefer. Set a rack over a roasting pan with 1 to 1/2 inches of water in it. Remove the ribs from the marinade and place them on the rack. Turn and baste them every 10 minutes during the cooking. Cook the ribs until they are done, about 30 to 40 minutes.

Makes 6 servings.

Barbecued Country-Style Pork Ribs

This flavorful recipe hails from California and adds a different twist to traditional barbecue. Make the sour cream sauce while the ribs are marinating so you can chill it before serving it alongside at the table.

1 cup red wine
1 cup red wine vinegar
1 carrot, peeled and grated
1 small onion, peeled and stuck with 3 whole cloves
1/4 teaspoon thyme
2 cloves garlic, minced
3 pounds country-style pork ribs, in individual pieces
1 teaspoon salt
Freshly ground black pepper to taste
1 recipe Sour Cream Sauce (recipe follows)

To Prepare the Marinade

Combine the red wine, red wine vinegar, carrot, onion, thyme, and garlic in a large glass or ceramic bowl.

To Barbecue the Ribs

Sprinkle the ribs with salt and black pepper and place them in the marinade, uncovered, for 2 hours at room temperature, or covered overnight in the refrigerator. Turn the ribs occasionally.

Preheat the oven for 15 minutes at 450°F (230°C). Remove the ribs from the marinade, reserving 1/2 cup for the Sour Cream Sauce. Put the ribs on a rack placed over a roasting pan and cook for 10 minutes per side. Remove the pan from the oven. Reduce the heat to 350°F (175°C). Spoon on the marinade, coating the ribs well. Return the pan to the oven.

Every 10 minutes, turn and baste the ribs. When the sauce forms a rich glaze (about 45 minutes), remove the ribs from the oven and transfer to a serving platter. Serve with the Sour Cream Sauce.

Sour Cream Sauce

2 Tablespoons unsalted butter
2 small onions, finely minced
1/2 cup reserved marinade
1/4 teaspoon freshly ground black pepper
3/4 cup sour cream, at room temperature
1/4 cup finely minced fresh parsley

Melt the butter in a small skillet over medium heat. Add the onions and sauté them until they are transparent. Add the marinade, increase the heat, and bring the mixture to a boil. Reduce the heat and simmer, uncovered, until the liquid is reduced by one-third. Add the black pepper and stir in the sour cream. Remove the mixture from the heat as soon as the sour cream is well incorporated (do *not* boil), and stir in the parsley. Refrigerate this sauce while you cook the ribs.

New England Maple Barbecued Pork

Tom Boyhan adds maple syrup to his winning sauce and uses it to marinate cubes of pork shoulder. Then the pork is combined on skewers with chunks of navel oranges and sections of bell peppers. The resulting kabobs won him the title of king at the 1979 New York State Pork Cookout. Make the sauce at least a day in advance of your barbecue. Keep it refrigerated in a covered container until you are ready to use it.

    2 cups ketchup
    1 1/2 cups pure maple syrup
    1/2 cup cider vinegar
    1/2 cup fresh orange juice
    2 Tablespoons Worcestershire sauce
    2 teaspoons salt
    2 Tablespoons minced onion
    1/2 teaspoon liquid smoke (optional)
    2 to 2 1/2 pounds boneless pork shoulder, cut in 1 1/2-inch cubes
    2 unpeeled navel oranges, cut in wedges
    3 green bell peppers, steamed, seeded, and cut in 1 1/2-inch cubes
    12 bamboo skewers, 7 to 8 inches long

TO PREPARE THE SAUCE

Combine ketchup, maple syrup, cider vinegar, orange juice, Worcestershire, salt, and onion in a 2-quart saucepan. Simmer, uncovered, over medium heat for 15 minutes. Add the liquid smoke, stir, and set aside in the refrigerator until you are ready to marinate the meat.

Makes 1 quart.

TO BARBECUE THE PORK

Place the pork cubes in a shallow glass bowl or baking dish. Pour the sauce over the cubes. Stir, making sure all sides of the meat are covered with the sauce. Marinate for 1 to 2 hours at room temperature or covered overnight in the refrigerator.

Preheat the oven to 450°F (230°C). On each skewer place a wedge of orange, then alternate with pork cubes and green pepper cubes. Place the kabobs on a rack in a shallow baking pan and roast in the oven (not the broiler) for 10 minutes, turning occasionally.

Reduce the heat to 350°F (175°C), baste the kabobs, and continue to cook for about 20 minutes, turning and basting again after 10 minutes. When done, the sauce will have formed a thick rich brown glaze.

Makes 6 servings.

Yankee Brisket Pulled Barbecue

A Yankee version of the famous pit-cooked pulled barbecue, this is a super prepare-ahead meal. Sylvia Carter, food writer for *Newsday* in New York, introduced me to this finger lickin' good recipe. Serve with steamed soft buns, large garlicky dill pickles, coleslaw, and baked beans. A word of warning: make lots! There is seldom any left. It is one of the best for large gatherings, as it waits patiently for buffet service and seems to somehow improve with the waiting.

    4 pounds beef brisket or chuck roast (pork shoulder may also be used)
    1 (3 1/2-ounce) bottle liquid smoke
    2 cups chopped onions
    1/4 cup cider vinegar
    1/4 cup firmly packed dark brown sugar
    2 Tablespoons Dusseldorf mustard or any spicy brown mustard or yellow mustard
    1 Tablespoon dark molasses
    1/4 teaspoon cayenne pepper
    1/4 teaspoon liquid hot pepper sauce
    3 Tablespoons Worcestershire sauce
    1 cup ketchup
    1/2 cup chili sauce (ketchup-style)
    1/2 lemon, sliced
    1 Tablespoon salt, more or less, to taste
    1/4 teaspoon freshly ground black pepper

Preheat the oven to 325°F (160°C). Put the meat on a rack in a roasting pan, fat side up, and pour the liquid smoke around it. Seal the pan with foil and place in the oven. Roast the brisket for 4 hours, or until it is very tender, turning once. Uncover the meat for the last 30 minutes to brown. Remove the meat from the oven and let it cool. Wrap it in plastic and refrigerate. Pour the pan juices and fat into a glass jar or bowl, cover, and refrigerate.

The next day remove the meat from the refrigerator and trim away any extra fat. Pull the meat into small shreds (this is called pulling). Remove the hardened fat from the pan juices.

In a large pot melt 3 Tablespoons of the hardened fat over medium heat, add the onions, and sauté until tender. Add cider vinegar, brown sugar, mustard, molasses, cayenne pepper, hot pepper sauce, Worcestershire, ketchup, chili sauce, lemon slices, salt, and black pepper, and 1 cup of the pan juices. Stir well and simmer for 20 minutes over low heat.

Add the pulled meat to the sauce and simmer very slowly, uncovered, for 1 hour, stirring frequently. Add more pan juices, or water, if necessary, to keep the meat moist.

Makes 8 to 12 servings.

Pulled Barbecue

This method prepares your meat for a delicious pulled barbecue. I prefer using beef brisket and beef round roasts, but pork shoulders and butts may be used. Here's how to do it in the oven or on top of the stove.

If you are cooking the meat in the oven, preheat it to 325°F (160°C). Sprinkle the meat with salt and pepper to taste. Place it in a heavy pot. If you intend to cook the meat on a burner, add 1/2 cup water to the pot and cover tightly with a lid or aluminum foil.

Cook on the lowest flame or heat setting possible. Check the meat periodically and add more water if necessary. If you are cooking the meat in the oven, you don't need to add water. Just cover tightly and place in the oven. For either method, cook approximately 1 hour per pound of meat, or until the meat is fork-tender and falls apart. When the meat is done, remove it from the pot and allow it to cool. Trim any excess fat from the meat.

For full pulled meat, pull meat into shreds with your hands or two forks. For partially pulled meat, pull the meat into 1-inch chunks. Return the shredded meat to the pot, add your favorite sauce, allowing 1/2 cup sauce per pound of meat or to taste, and cook, uncovered, over low heat. The barbecue should be heated through.

Texas Beef Barbecue

"Texas class" all the way! I love to serve it with the sauce used in James Beal's Barbecued Ribs, page 15, but you can use your own favorite with it. Serve the meat charred but rare for a true Texas taste.

    4 pounds top beef round, well-trimmed
    1/4 cup lard, divided
    1/2 teaspoon chile caribe (crushed red chile)
    1/2 cup boiling water
    1/2 cup (1 stick) unsalted butter
    1/2 cup tarragon vinegar, or 1/2 cup cider vinegar plus 1 Tablespoon fresh or 1 teaspoon dried
        tarragon
    1 1/2 cups dry red wine
    1/3 cup freshly grated onion
    2 Tablespoons Worcestershire sauce
    1 large clove garlic, minced

Wipe the meat with a damp cloth, then rub it with 1/8 cup of the lard and the chile caribe. In a 1-quart saucepan boil the water. Add the remaining 1/8 cup lard and all the butter. Allow them to melt, then add the tarragon vinegar, red wine, onion, Worcestershire, and garlic and stir to mix.

Place the meat in a medium-size bowl, and pour the sauce over it. Let the meat stand in the liquid for 4 hours at room temperature, or for 2 days, covered, in the refrigerator. Turn the meat from time to time so both sides absorb the marinade.

Preheat the broiler. Remove the meat from the marinade and place it on the broiler pan. Position the pan on the bottom rack of the broiler, as far as possible from the broiling unit, so the surface of the meat is 3 to 4 inches from the heat. Broil the meat for 15 minutes. Turn the meat and baste it generously with marinade, rubbing the fat from the marinade over the surface of the meat. Broil another 15 minutes. Turn the meat and baste again thoroughly. Broil 15 minutes. At this point the meat will be rare. Baste the meat, remove it from the oven, and allow it to rest for 15 minutes.

If a more well-done roast is desired, reduce the oven temperature to 325°F (160°C), and cook the roast in the oven for an additional 30 to 60 minutes, depending on the doneness preferred. Serve with your choice of sauce at the table.

Makes 6 to 8 servings.

Note: If a broiler is not available, roast the meat in a preheated 450°F (230°C) oven for 30 minutes, basting frequently. Turn the meat, reduce the temperature to 325°F (160°C), and cook for 2 hours, basting every 20 minutes, or until the meat tests done with a meat thermometer (internal temperature of 150°F, 65°C).

Amy's Sloppy Joe's

My daughter, Amy, and her friends have made these a frequent request. Spicy and saucy, this meat is wonderful on fresh, soft whole-wheat buns.

    1 pound lean ground beef, cold or at room temperature
    1/4 cup finely diced onion
    1 clove garlic, minced
    1/4 cup ketchup
    2 teaspoons pure ground mild red chile
    1 teaspoon prepared yellow mustard
    1 teaspoon Worcestershire sauce
    1/4 teaspoon liquid smoke (optional)
    1/2 teaspoon celery salt
    6 fresh whole-wheat hamburger buns

In a large skillet crumble the hamburger and cook over medium heat. As it cooks, add the onion, garlic, ketchup, ground chile, mustard, Worcestershire, liquid smoke, and celery salt, stirring to mix well with the hamburger. When thoroughly cooked, spoon onto toasted whole-wheat hamburger buns and serve.

Makes 6 sandwiches.

Jerry's Beef Barbecue

Since Jerry Wood feels that beef requires a different sauce from chicken or pork, I have added another of his favorites.

1 cup beef broth
3 cups ketchup
1/2 cup cider vinegar
1/4 cup Worcestershire sauce
1/4 cup firmly packed light brown sugar
2 teaspoons salt or to taste
1 teaspoon liquid smoke (optional)
1 (4 1/2 to 6-pound) chuck roast

To Prepare the Sauce

In a 2-quart saucepan combine broth, ketchup, cider vinegar, Worcestershire, brown sugar, and salt, and bring to a simmer over medium heat. Reduce the heat to low and cook, uncovered, 30 minutes, until slightly thickened. Add the liquid smoke, if desired. Set the sauce aside to cool.

Makes 1 quart.

To Roast the Beef

In a large roasting pan marinate the roast in the sauce for 2 hours at room temperature. Turn the meat after an hour.

Preheat the oven to 325°F (160°C). Remove the meat from the marinade and wipe off any extra sauce. Reserve the marinade. Place the meat in a clean casserole or roasting pan, cover it tightly (using foil if necessary), and cook for 3 1/2 hours or until it is very tender. After 2 hours, turn the roast.

Uncover the meat and cook for another 30 minutes, basting with the reserved marinade, until it is nice and brown. Remove the roast from the pan, allow it to cool for 15 minutes, then slice it thin, and serve..

Makes 6 to 8 servings.

Jane's Special Sweet and Sour Chicken

This is one of the best summer weekend dishes around. The sauce is terrific as well as quick and easy to prepare. Serve this chicken with a creamy coleslaw (see recipe on page 53) and foil-wrapped, grill-roasted corn on the cob.

3/4 cup ketchup
3/4 cup apricot preserves
2 Tablespoons white or cider vinegar
1 teaspoon Worcestershire sauce
1 Tablespoon pure ground mild red chile
1/2 teaspoon salt
3 to 4 pounds chicken, cut into serving pieces

To Prepare the Sauce

In a 2-quart saucepan combine ketchup, apricot preserves, vinegar, Worcestershire, ground chile, and salt and cook over medium heat until the mixture comes to a boil. Stir the sauce occasionally to prevent it from sticking. Reduce the heat to low and simmer, uncovered, for 5 minutes. Set the sauce aside until you are ready to cook the chicken—or once it has cooled, marinate the chicken in the sauce for 1 to 2 hours at room temperature for even better flavor.

Makes 1 1/2 cups.

To Barbecue the Chicken

Adjust the broiler rack so that the chicken will be 3 to 4 inches from the heat. Preheat the broiler. Lay the chicken pieces on the rack of a broiler, skin side up. (If you want, cover the rack with heavy-duty broiler foil punctured with holes.) Broil for 20 minutes.

Turn the chicken, baste it with the sauce, and cook for 15 minutes. Then turn and baste again. Baste and turn every 5 minutes until the chicken is done, another 15 to 25 minutes.

Makes 2 servings.

Sweet Southern Chicken

Mississippians like barbecue too! This recipe has a sweet, savory, tart taste—it's the lemon that makes it special. Given to me by a highly respected friend in the fine-food field, I bet you will want to add this one to your "favorites" file. Once you're hooked, you'll want to try it on other meats. It's good on fish as well!

1 cup ketchup
2 Tablespoons honey
3 Tablespoons lemon juice
1 Tablespoon Worcestershire sauce
4 large cloves garlic, finely minced
4 Tablespoons bacon drippings
1 small lemon, sliced thin and seeds removed
Liquid hot pepper sauce to taste
Salt and freshly ground black pepper to taste
1/2 teaspoon liquid smoke (optional)
3 pounds chicken, cut into serving pieces

To Prepare the Sauce

In a 2-quart enamel saucepan combine ketchup, honey, lemon juice, Worcestershire, garlic, bacon drippings, lemon slices, hot pepper sauce, salt, and black pepper and bring to a boil over medium-high heat, stirring occasionally. When it is thoroughly blended, in about 20 minutes, add the liquid smoke and set the sauce aside until you are ready to cook the chicken. Or for even better flavor, marinate the chicken in the sauce for 1 to 2 hours at room temperature.

Makes 1 1/2 cups.

To Barbecue the Chicken

Adjust the broiler rack of your oven so that the surface of the chicken will be 3 to 4 inches from the heat. Preheat the broiler. Lay the chicken pieces on the rack of a broiler pan, skin side up. (If you want, cover the rack with heavy-duty broiler foil punctured with holes.) Broil for 20 minutes.

Turn the chicken, baste it with the sauce, and cook for 15 minutes. Then turn it and baste again. Baste and turn every 5 minutes until the chicken is done, in another 15 to 25 minutes.

Makes 2 to 3 servings.

Addie's Texas Barbecued Chicken

This dish is from deep in the heart of Texas. My favorite sister-in-law treated me to it for the first time more than twenty years ago, and to this day I think it's the best. Addie, who hailed from Arkansas as a kid, says the secret is in using the unsalted butter and the freshest possible ingredients. Addie also introduced me to her famous potato salad. I still make her potato salad and have included her recipe on page 54. All you need with this barbecued chicken and Addie's potato salad is a relish tray. Then just sit back and wait for compliments.

1/2 cup cider vinegar
2 Tablespoons firmly packed light brown sugar
1 Tablespoon prepared yellow mustard
1 1/2 teaspoons salt or to taste
1/2 teaspoon freshly ground black pepper
2 Tablespoons fresh lemon juice
1 cup finely diced onion
1/2 cup (1 stick) unsalted butter, cut into 6 pieces
1 (15-ounce) can tomato sauce
2 Tablespoons Worcestershire sauce
1 1/2 teaspoons liquid smoke (optional)
1 1/2 teaspoons dried sage or 1/2 teaspoon fresh sage, minced
1 1/2 teaspoons basil or 1/2 teaspoon fresh basil, minced
1 1/2 teaspoons rosemary or 1/2 teaspoon fresh rosemary, minced
1 1/2 teaspoons thyme or 1/2 teaspoon fresh thyme, minced
6 pounds chicken, cut into serving pieces

To Prepare the Sauce

In a 2-quart saucepan combine the cider vinegar, brown sugar, mustard, salt, black pepper, lemon, onion, and butter. Bring the mixture to a boil over high heat. Reduce the heat to medium and simmer for 20 minutes, uncovered. Stir occasionally.

Add the tomato sauce, Worcestershire, and liquid smoke, if using. Simmer for 15 minutes longer, again stirring occasionally. Add the sage, basil, rosemary, and thyme, reduce the heat to low, and cook the sauce for 5 minutes. Remove the sauce from the heat, cool, cover, and refrigerate until you are ready to barbecue.

Makes 3 1/2 cups.

To Barbecue the Chicken

Adjust the broiler rack of your oven so the chicken will be 4 inches from the heat. Preheat the broiler. Lay the chicken pieces on the rack of a broiler pan, skin side up. (If you want, cover the rack with heavy-duty broiler foil punctured with holes.) Broil for 20 minutes.

Turn the chicken, baste it with the sauce, and cook for 15 minutes. Then turn it and baste again. Baste and turn every 5 minutes until the chicken is done, another 15 to 25 minutes.

Makes 6 servings.

Note: As a sauce variation, omit the herbs and add 3 whole green chiles, finely chopped, 1/4 teaspoon ground ginger, 1/4 teaspoon ground cinnamon, and several drops of liquid hot pepper sauce or to taste.

Orange Barbecued Ham

This sweet sauce is terrific on poultry as well as ham. A salad of peeled sliced oranges and red onions served on lettuce leaves with poppy-seed/honey dressing along with baked sweet potatoes would make the perfect meal. A bone-in, ready-to-eat ham should be cooked at 14 minutes per pound. A boneless ham will take longer—30 minutes per pound.

1/2 cup honey
1/2 cup dry red wine
2 teaspoons freshly grated orange rind
1/2 cup freshly squeezed orange juice
2 teaspoons unsalted butter
2 teaspoons snipped chives
Salt and freshly ground black pepper to taste
1 (5 to 7-pound) ready-to-eat ham

To Prepare the Sauce

In a 2-quart enamel saucepan combine honey, red wine, grated orange rind, orange juice, butter, chives, salt, and black pepper and cook, uncovered, over medium heat for 20 minutes. Set aside until you are ready to cook the ham.

Makes 1 3/4 cups.

To Barbecue the Ham

Preheat the oven to 400°F (205°C). Place the ham in a large roasting pan and then in the oven. After 20 minutes, reduce the heat to 325°F (160°C). After another 30 minutes, start basting the ham at 20-minute intervals. After 2 hours roasting time, remove the ham from the oven. Cut off the rind and all but 1/4 inch of fat; score the fat and baste with the sauce. Return the ham to the oven and baste every 5 minutes until done.

Makes 10 to 12 servings.

Mustard Barbecued Ham

One regional sauce, popular with the western South Carolinians, is this mustard-base version.

3/4 cup water
3 Tablespoons finely minced onion
1 medium clove garlic, finely minced
1 cup prepared yellow mustard
1 teaspoon dry mustard
3 Tablespoons chile sauce (ketchup-style)
2 Tablespoons plus 1 teaspoon sugar
2 teaspoons honey
1 Tablespoon Worcestershire sauce
1/8 teaspoon freshly ground white pepper
1/4 teaspoon freshly ground black pepper
1/2 teaspoon pure ground hot red chile
1 (5- to 7-pound) ready-to-eat ham

TO PREPARE THE SAUCE

In a 2-quart saucepan place the water, onion, and garlic, and bring to a boil over medium heat. Reduce the heat to low and add the prepared mustard, dry mustard, chile sauce, sugar, honey, Worcestershire, white pepper, black pepper, and ground chile, whisking thoroughly to combine. Continue to cook for 15 minutes. Remove the sauce from the heat. If you wish to refrigerate it, let it cool.

Makes 2 cups.

TO BARBECUE THE HAM

Preheat the oven to 400°F (205°C). Place the ham in a large roasting pan and then in the oven. After 20 minutes, reduce the heat to 325°F (160°C). After another 30 minutes, start basting the ham at 20-minute intervals.

Forty-five minutes before the cooking time is up, remove the ham from the oven. Cut off the rind and all but 1/4 inch of fat; score the fat and baste with the sauce. Return the ham to the oven and baste every 5 minutes until it's done. A bone-in, ready-to-eat ham should be cooked 14 minutes per pound. A boneless ham will take longer—30 minutes per pound.

Makes 10 to 12 servings.

Steve's Bermuda Lamb

Steve Mandler, an enthusiastic cook living in San Francisco, claims he created this dish from memories of many fabulous barbecues in Bermuda. There many of the cooks keep "hot" wine in the refrigerator for flavoring sauces. (To make "hot" wine, see the note below.)

    1/2 cup honey
    1/4 cup firmly packed brown sugar
    3/4 cup bottled chili sauce (ketchup-style)
    3 Tablespoons Worcestershire sauce
    1/2 teaspoon finely minced garlic
    1/4 cup minced onion
    1/2 cup flat beer
    1/4 teaspoon cayenne or "hot" wine*
    4 pounds lamb riblets

To Prepare the Sauce

In a heavy 1-quart saucepan combine honey, brown sugar, chili sauce, Worcestershire, garlic, onion, beer, and cayenne pepper (or "hot" wine). Bring the mixture to a boil over low heat and simmer, uncovered, for 10 minutes. Set the sauce aside until you are ready to barbecue the lamb.

Makes 2 cups.

*To make "hot" wine, steep 1/4 cup crushed red chile peppers in 1/2 cup red wine for 3 days in the refrigerator. Substitute 1 teaspoon of this wine for the cayenne pepper.

To Barbecue the Lamb

Preheat the oven to 450°F (230°C). Place the riblets on a rack in a shallow baking pan and sear 10 minutes on each side. (You can line the rack with heavy-duty broiler foil, if you like. Puncture plenty of holes in it for ventilation.) Reduce the heat to 350°F (175°C), baste the riblets with the sauce, and continue cooking for between 20 to 30 minutes, basting and turning every 10 minutes.

Makes 4 servings.

Big Fish Barbecue

Up North, most anyone worth having fun with loves barbecue as much as Southerners do. I like using this northern sauce on fish best of all.

2 Tablespoons vegetable oil
2 cups finely chopped onions
1/2 cup chicken or beef stock
1 cup peeled and chopped fresh tomatoes or canned Italian plum tomatoes
4 Tablespoons freshly squeezed lemon juice
3 Tablespoons light brown sugar
3 Tablespoons Worcestershire sauce
2 Tablespoons dry mustard
1 Tablespoon salt
Freshly ground black pepper to taste
Dash of liquid hot pepper sauce
3 to 4 pounds fresh fish steaks such as halibut, salmon, or swordfish, 1 inch thick

To Prepare the Sauce

Place the oil in a 1-quart saucepan over medium heat. Add the onions and sauté them until they are transparent. Add the chicken or beef stock, tomatoes, lemon juice, brown sugar, Worcestershire, mustard, salt, black pepper, and hot pepper sauce and bring the mixture to a boil. Lower the heat and simmer about 30 minutes. Set the sauce aside until you are ready to barbecue.

Makes 1 3/4 cups.

To Barbecue the Fish

Preheat the broiler and position the rack 5 inches below the heat source. Line a broiling pan with aluminum foil. Place the fish in the broiling pan and set it on the broiler rack. Allow the fish to cook 1 minute, then turn it. Spoon on the sauce. Broil for 4 minutes. Then turn the fish again and sauce the second side.

Fish cooks quickly and will fall apart if turned too many times, so do not turn the steaks more than twice. They should take no longer than 10 to 12 minutes. The fish is cooked when it flakes easily with a fork.

Makes 6 to 8 servings.

San Francisco Barbecued Fish

A sweet-tart, slightly smoky sauce to serve with any full-flavored fish such as trout, sturgeon, or tuna.

2 (1/4-inch-thick) slices of slab bacon, cut into narrow strips and diced
2 medium onions, finely chopped
3 large cloves garlic, minced
16 ounces tomato sauce
6 Tablespoons firmly packed brown sugar
1/4 cup white wine vinegar
4 Tablespoons plus 2 teaspoons fresh lemon juice
10 ounces flat beer
1 Tablespoon Worcestershire sauce
1 1/2 Tablespoons tamari or soy sauce
1 teaspoon ground ginger
1 teaspoon ground allspice
1 teaspoon freshly ground nutmeg
1 teaspoon celery seed
1/2 teaspoon cayenne pepper or pequin quebrado, more or less to taste
1 Tablespoon liquid smoke (optional)
Salt to taste
2 1/2 pounds any of the above fish fillets or 3 to 4 pounds baby red snapper, whole

TO PREPARE THE SAUCE

In a skillet sauté the bacon over medium heat until the fat is transparent. Add the onions and garlic and continue cooking until the onion is softened but not browned. Transfer this mixture to a 2-quart saucepan and add the tomato sauce, brown sugar, white wine vinegar, lemon juice, beer, Worcestershire, tamari or soy sauce, ginger, allspice, nutmeg, celery seed, and cayenne pepper.

Bring the mixture to the boiling point over medium heat. Reduce the heat to low and simmer, uncovered, for 30 minutes. Turn off the heat, add the liquid smoke, if desired, stir, and let the sauce cool. Taste, add salt, and adjust the seasonings. Set the sauce aside until you are ready to barbecue the fish.

Makes 3 1/2 cups.

TO BARBECUE THE FISH

Preheat the oven to 450°F (230°C). Place the oven rack 4 to 6 inches from the top of the oven. Line a shallow baking pan with foil. Place the fish in the pan and cook in the oven for 5 minutes before basting with the sauce. Baste the fish with the sauce occasionally, but only turn the fish once. Cook for 10 minutes per inch of thickness.

Makes 4 to 6 servings.

Note: You can also broil the fish. Just be sure it doesn't cook too quickly and dry out.

Accompaniments

A collection of just-the-right dishes to serve up with your favorite barbecued meat or fish. Then for a blissful ending to the feast, a super-rich fudge or Texas Pecan Cake. Who could ask for anything more?

Chuckwagon Salad

Great picnic fare, but don't dress the salad until it's time to eat.

  1 clove garlic, cut in half
  3 cups lettuce (preferably two or three types, for example a combination of romaine, watercress, and red leaf), torn into bite-size pieces
  2 stalks celery, thinly sliced
  Half a cucumber, peeled and thinly sliced
  2 medium ripe tomatoes, cut in wedges
  2 hardboiled large eggs, sliced and diced
  1 cup large lima beans, cooked and thoroughly drained (1/2 cup dry)
  1/4 cup blue-veined cheese, crumbled
  1/4 cup olive oil
  2 Tablespoons white wine vinegar
  1 teaspoon salad herbs—a combination of thyme, tarragon, and sweet basil
  Salt and freshly ground black pepper to taste

Rub a wooden salad bowl with the cut garlic, then discard the garlic. Add the lettuce, celery, cucumber, tomatoes, eggs, and lima beans to the bowl. Blend the cheese, oil, and white wine vinegar together and pour the mixture over the salad ingredients. Toss lightly and season with the herbs and salt and black pepper, to taste. Serve immediately.

Makes 4 to 6 servings.

Kay's Lexington Barbecue Slaw

To Kay Goldstein, a native of Lexington, North Carolina, now living in Georgia, "Lexington barbecue sauce *is* barbecue sauce." In Lexington, barbecue coleslaw is famous and is served with and on everything.

1 medium (2 1/2 to 3 pounds) head white cabbage
3 Tablespoons sugar
1 cup cider vinegar
2/3 cup ketchup
1/2 cup water
1/8 teaspoon cayenne pepper
1/8 teaspoon chile caribe (crushed red chile)
1/4 teaspoon freshly ground black pepper
3/4 teaspoon salt or to taste
Dash of liquid hot pepper sauce or to taste

Grate or thinly slice the cabbage. If you won't be using it for a while, you can keep the cabbage crisp by placing it in cold water to cover for several hours, or until needed. Drain well before using.

In a small saucepan combine the sugar and cider vinegar and cook over medium heat until the sugar dissolves. Whisk in the ketchup, water, cayenne pepper, chile, black pepper, salt, and hot pepper sauce, and simmer over medium-high heat for 10 minutes. If the mixture seems too thick, thin with 1 Tablespoon of warm water at a time until the proper consistency is reached. Pour the warm sauce over the grated cabbage. Toss to combine thoroughly, and serve immediately.

Makes 6 servings.

Texas Potato Salad

This recipe came to me by way of my sister-in-law, Addie. Once you try it, you'll never go back to your old recipe . . . 'cause this one's fantastic!

    4 medium-size baking potatoes (Idaho or Russet), unpeeled
    2 teaspoons salt
    2 large eggs
    2 Tablespoons vinegar
    3 Tablespoons unsalted butter
    4 Tablespoons finely diced Spanish onion
    6 Tablespoons finely diced sweet gherkins
    3 Tablespoons juice from the sweet gherkins
    1/2 cup mayonnaise
    1 whole canned pimiento, sliced into 1/4-inch strips
    1 whole sweet gherkin

Over medium heat in a covered saucepan, cook the potatoes in water to cover mixed with 1 teaspoon of the salt until they are fork-tender, about 20 minutes. Remove the pan from the heat, drain the potatoes, and replace the lid, allowing the potatoes to steam for 15 minutes.

Meanwhile, cook the eggs with the vinegar and the remaining 1 teaspoon salt in water to cover, until just done, about 10 minutes. Drain and run cold water over them to cool. Peel, then slice and dice the eggs.

Peel the potatoes and return them to the cooking pot. Add the butter to the pot, cutting through the potatoes with a sharp knife to allow the butter to be absorbed. The potatoes should be in rough, medium-size chunks. Cover the pot and allow them to stand, off the heat, for 10 minutes. If the potatoes are not hot enough to melt the butter, place the pot, covered, over low heat for a few minutes.

Off the heat, add the diced eggs, onion, diced gherkins, gherkin juice, and mayonnaise and mix thoroughly. Transfer the mixture to your favorite bowl, garnish with sliced pimiento, and place the whole gherkin in the center.

Makes 4 to 6 servings.

Barbecued Baked Beans

The combination of flavors makes this my favorite baked-bean recipe of all time.

    4 slices lean bacon, cut crosswise into thin strips
    1 cup finely diced Spanish onion
    1 large clove garlic, minced
    1 pound cooked navy or pea beans, or 1 (16-ounce) can brick-oven baked beans
    3/4 cup ketchup
    1 cup firmly packed dark brown sugar
    1 teaspoon dry mustard
    1 Tablespoon pure ground mild red chile

Preheat the oven to 325°F (160°C). In a heavy skillet sauté the bacon strips over medium-high heat until crisp. Add the onion and garlic, and continue cooking until the onion is transparent but not browned.

Transfer the bacon, onion, garlic, and any fat that may have accumulated to a bowl. Add the beans, ketchup, brown sugar, mustard, and ground chile and combine well. Pour the mixture into an ungreased 2-quart baking dish and bake uncovered at 325°F (160°C) for 2 1/2 to 3 hours.

Makes 4 servings.

Note: The beans will up to 2 weeks in refrigerator, but don't freeze them; freezing tends to change the texture and make the beans mushy.

Corn on the Cob

This is the best possible way to cook and serve fresh corn! Try it once and you'll be hooked for life.

4 ears fresh corn, husks and silk intact
2 gallons salted water

If the corn is more than 2 hours from the stalk, soak it in salted water for 10 to 20 minutes before placing it on your outdoor grill. About 20 minutes before your meal is ready to be served, place the ears of corn on the grill, rotating them frequently. The husks will get slightly charred.

Corn is done when the kernels emit water when pierced with the point of a sharp knife or a fork, in about 15 to 20 minutes. Husk corn (be careful, it's still hot!) and serve immediately.

Makes 4 servings.

Note: If corn fresh off the stalk is not available, the flavor of "tired" corn can be freshened by cooking the husked corn in a solution of 2 Tablespoons sugar, 1/2 teaspoon salt, and 1/4 cup dried milk to each cup of water. Drain the corn well before serving.

Barbecued Cheese

This tasty cheese dish bears a similarity to Swiss Raclette, which is the name both of a cheese and of the dish in which it is cooked. A wheel of Raclette is placed in a cast-iron skillet and a metal spike is inserted in the cheese to hold it steady. The skillet is placed over the fire and as the cheese slowly melts, it is scraped from the pan wheel with a sharp knife and served with fresh homemade bread or crackers.

1/2 wheel Raclette or Appenzell cheese
1/4 cup virgin olive oil
1 to 2 teaspoons dried oregano

Brush the wheel of cheese with the olive oil and sprinkle with the oregano. Place the cheese on a solid griddle or in a large cast-iron frying pan over an open fire, a grill, or a fire pit. If you are cooking indoors, place the griddle on a burner over medium heat. As the cheese melts, scrape it into the pan with a wooden knife or spatula, adding more oil and oregano if needed. Serve the cheese directly from the pan on hot fresh bread and accompany it with red wine.

Makes 10 servings.

Norma Jean's Hush Puppies

These hush puppies, a recipe from McEwen, Tennessee, are sheer heaven, the best I've ever encountered. When camping, I've even taken the dry ingredients mixed together so I could whip them up in the woods. They're terrific with any kind of barbecue.

1 quart peanut oil, for frying hush puppies
2 cups white cornmeal
1 Tablespoon all-purpose flour
1/2 teaspoon baking soda
1 teaspoon baking powder
2 teaspoons sugar
1 1/2 teaspoons salt
1 cup buttermilk
1 small onion, finely minced
1 large egg, beaten

In a deep-fat fryer, preheat oil to 375°F (190°C). In a large bowl combine cornmeal, flour, baking soda, baking powder, sugar, salt, buttermilk, and onion. Then add the egg. Mix well and drop a tablespoonful at a time into the hot fat. Do not overcrowd.

When done, in about 3 minutes, the hush puppies will turn golden brown and float to the top. Remove them from the oil with a slotted spoon or tongs and drain thoroughly on paper towels. Serve the hush puppies warm.

Makes 24 1-inch hush puppies.

Fudge Cake

My mother-in-law always served this cake for special occasions. It's a phenomenal ending to a barbecue. The date cream filling complements its rich fudge flavor.

3/4 cup (1 1/2 sticks) unsalted butter, softened
2 1/4 cups sugar
3 large eggs
3 squares of unsweetened chocolate, melted over low heat and cooled
1 1/2 teaspoons vanilla extract
2 1/4 teaspoons baking soda
3/4 teaspoon salt
3 cups all-purpose flour
1 1/2 cups ice water
Date Cream Filling (recipe follows)

Preheat the oven to 350°F (175°C). Cream together the butter and sugar in the bowl of a mixer. Add the eggs, incorporating them one at a time into the batter, and beat until thick and fluffy. Add the cooled chocolate and the vanilla. Sift together the baking soda, salt, and flour and add them to the batter alternately with the ice water.

Grease thoroughly three 8-inch round layer pans and line the bottoms with circles of waxed paper cut to fit. Divide the batter evenly among the pans and bake for 30 to 35 minutes. To test for doneness, insert a toothpick in the center of each layer. If it comes out clean and dry, the cake is done.

Remove the pans from the oven and let them cool on cake racks. Turn the cake out of the pans after 10 minutes' cooling time.

In the meantime, make the filling. Place the first cake layer on a plate and smooth on one-third of the filling. Add the next layer, spread one-third of the filling over it, and top with the third layer. Spread the remaining filling over the top. This cake is best when served while still warm.

DATE CREAM FILLING
2 cups milk
1 cup chopped pitted dates
1/2 cup sugar
2 Tablespoons all-purpose flour
2 large eggs
2 teaspoons vanilla extract
1 cup chopped pecans, or your favorite nuts

Place the milk and dates in a small saucepan and warm them over low heat. Meanwhile, in a small bowl combine the sugar and flour. In another small bowl beat the eggs and then add them to the sugar-flour mixture. Gradually add this mixture to the hot milk and dates. Cook the filling until it thickens enough to coat a spoon, about 15 minutes. Then stir in the vanilla and nuts.

Makes 8 servings.

Texas Pecan Cake

My Dallas buddies gave me this recipe years ago. It's perfectly outrageous served after barbecue, and quite frankly, it's wonderful anytime.

1 pound (4 sticks) unsalted butter, softened
2 cups sugar
6 large eggs, well beaten
1 teaspoon lemon extract
4 cups unbleached all-purpose flour
1 1/2 teaspoons baking powder
4 cups pecan halves
2 cups white raisins
Powdered sugar (optional)

Preheat the oven to 300°F (150°C). Grease and lightly flour a 9 3/4-inch tube pan. Shake out any excess flour from the pan.

With a mixer or by hand, blend the butter and sugar together in a large bowl; beat until the mixture is light and fluffy. Gradually add the eggs and lemon extract, and beat well. Sift the flour and baking powder together three times; add the nuts and raisins.

Gradually add the flour mixture to the creamed mixture and blend well. Pour the batter into the tube pan. Bake 1 1/2 to 2 hours, or until a cake tester comes out clean. Cool the cake for 15 minutes, then remove it from the pan. Serve it dusted with powdered sugar, if desired.

Makes 8 to 10 servings.

PIT STOPS

Barbecue gets into your blood. Once you're hooked, you will do darn near anything to keep up the habit. And a large part of the fun is in discovering a great new restaurant. In my travels I have developed a dear-to-my-heart list of the best pit stops, and here are some of the best. Barbecue has continued to become amazingly popular all over the country with many of the favorite pit stops in my original book growing more popular or new ones springing up. I have done my best to update my list to include many of the outstanding locations you can find throughout the United States. There are also a large number of barbecue competitions where individuals and restaurants showcase their best. The epicenter of barbecue seems to be the triad of Austin, Texas; to Kansas City, Kansas and Missouri; to Memphis and Nashville, Tennessee.

A great many of the following places and even more are offering online ordering of their meats, sauces, and side dishes. Check out their websites for ordering information, and most of all, ENJOY!

MIGHTY QUINN'S

1492 2nd Avenue
New York, New York 10075
(646) 484-5691
mightyquinnsbbq.com
Multiple locations in New York City and New Jersey

A relative newcomer, Mighty Quinn's is part of the all-wood-burning Renaissance flourishing among the elite barbecue restaurants. Using the best farm-sourced, all-natural poultry and meat products, meats are treated simply with salt, pepper, and paprika and allowed to cook a full 22 hours in a pit with oak and fruitwood embers. Quinn's pairs this painstaking 'cue with less traditional, creative side dishes like grilled ratatouille, sweet pea salads, and a bevy of pickled items like celery, onions, and chiles.

BLUE SMOKE

116 East 27th Street
New York, New York 10016
(212) 447-7733

255 Vesey Street
New York, New York 10282
(212) 889-2005
bluesmoke.com

Founded by the Danny Meyers Union Square Hospitality Group, Blue Smoke features Southern-style barbeque. The food is so popular, they have a growing group of baseball park and airport locations. They have taken the Alabama sourced White Wings to a new level featuring the Alabama famed mayonnaise-vinegar–based sauce.

JOEPER'S SMOKESHACK

2085 Flatbush Avenue
Brooklyn, New York 11234
(718) 677-4225
joeperssmokeshack.net

This Tennessee barbeque–inspired place was developed by Joe Pandolfo in 2011. He features dry rub smoked ribs that he serves with three different sauces.

John Brown's Smokehouse

10-43 44th Drive
Long Island City, New York 11101
(347) 617-11101
johnbrownseriousbbq.com

Also fairly new in the New York City area is this Kansas City–style barbecue place just over the Queen's Bridge, which opened in 2010. It features a very popular Kansas City favorite, "burnt ends," made famous by Joe's KC in Kansas City. They are the ends of dry rubbed brisket heavily smoked. Their cornbread is also a favorite.

Tony Romas, A Place for Ribs

3 Newark Airport Terminal A,
Space A12
Newark, New Jersey 07114
(973) 854-0891

4304 Palisades Center Drive
West Nack, New York 10994
(845) 353-8669
tonyromas.com

Tony Roma's rib houses got their start in 1972 in Miami and are located in 150 major cities in the USA and 27 other countries. Most assuredly, the secret of their success lies in the fun atmosphere, the long serving hours, and the great value of high-quality fast food, cooked to order. Favorites are the St. Louis–style baby back ribs and the onion loaf appetizer.

Fletcher's Brooklyn Barbecue

433 Third Avenue
Brooklyn, New York 11215

F, G, R trains @ 4th Avenue and 9th Street
(347) 763-2680
fletchersbklyn.com

At Fletcher's you will find a crowd-pleasing array of regional BBQ styles from the white sauces of the South to a Carolina vinegar-based sauce. Fletcher's embraces the multicultural environment of its home in Brooklyn, and you will find interesting intersections of flavored such as pit-cooked Chinese char sui pork sharing the menu with the standard southern BBQ dessert of banana pudding. But be assured, this 50-seat counter service restaurant is very serious about its technique, employing only wood fire in its pit cooking and sourcing the best in sustainable beef and pork.

BRANDED '72

387 East Gude Drive
Rockville, Maryland 20850
(301) 340-8596
branded72.com

Branded '72, formerly called O'Briens, was started in 1972 as a Texas-style pit barbeque restaurant. O'Brien's main location is near Washington, DC. Owner Ken O'Brien specializes in beef brisket hickory smoked over an inside pit. He also serves pork ribs and the standard accompaniments—slaw, baked beans, potato salad, corn on the cob, and chili.

ROCKLANDS BBQ AND GRILLING COMPANY

2418 Wisconsin Avenue NW
Washington, DC 20007
(202) 333-2558
(as well as locations in Virginia and Maryland)
rocklands.com

Barbecue fit for the president, Rocklands was charged with catering duties for Bill Clinton's first state dinner way back in 1993. Rocklands threw its doors open over 25 years ago and never looked back. Eschewing the convenience of gas and electric cooking, Rocklands smokes only with hickory and red oak, giving its meat a unique true smoke flavor.

CARNIVORE BBQ

1 Millionaire Drive
Bethesda, Maryland
(240) 53-BBQ4U
carnbbq.com

Carnivore owns and operates four BBQ food trucks in the DC area, as well as a central smokehouse location for dine-in or carry-out. Starting with one truck (lovingly called "Old Smokey" after its handcrafted smoker rig), it's not hard to see why Carnivore has become such a success in DC with its crowd-pleasing core of smoked chicken, brisket, and pulled pork. Carnivore is a part of the new school BBQ joints only utilizing wood fire cooking, and it shows through in their hours as this is some of the finest barbecue in not only Chicago, but the whole country.

THE GOLDEN RULE

2506 Crestwood Boulevard
Irondale, Alabama 35210
(205) 956-2678

One of the best-known barbecues in Alabama, founded in 1891 as a pit stop for travelers going to and from Atlanta, Georgia, it has evolved into a full-scale restaurant that is the longest continuously operating restaurant in Alabama. The Golden Rule now has five franchise locations throughout the Southeast. All the locations specialize in smoked pork and pork ribs and also serve beef and chicken. The sauce is the key to their success, along with the fact that they pit-smoke indoors with hickory wood. They are credited with creating the now famous "white sauce" for barbequed chicken wings.

SONNY'S BBQ

2700 North Waldo Road
Gainesville, Florida 32609
(352) 378-7881
sonnysbbq.com

Floyd "Sonny" Tillman originated this restaurant in 1968, and sold it to Bov Yarmuth in 1991. There are now over 150 locations in 9 southern state featuring pork ribs, sliced beef, and chicken. They use a basting sauce specifically formulated for use during cooking. A separate sauce is served at the table. Smoking over their open pits and using only black jack oak makes the barbecue at Sonny's especially tasty.

THE SMOKEY PIG BAR-B-Q

2520 Louisville Road
Bowling Green, Kentucky 42101
(270) 781-1712
smokeypigbbq.com

Founded in 1969, Smoky Pig continues to be operated by the Huffer family, who bought it in 1999. You really can taste the hickory smoke in the chopped and sliced pork cooked in an indoor pit. And the barbecue beans are the best! The restaurant continues to receive rave reviews and won the Pig and the Pint BBQ contest.

SCOTT'S BAR-B-QUE
2734 Hemingway Highway
Hemingway, South Carolina 29554
(843) 558-0134
thescottsbbq.com

Many rate this barbeque restaurant in the middle of nowhere one of the best places they have eaten—it features the South Carolina vinegar-based sauce and pulled pork. Be aware: it's very hot and spicy, yet a real favorite. Many also like their chicken and sauce.

LEXINGTON BARBECUE
100 Smokehouse Lane
Lexington, North Carolina 27295
(336) 249-9814
lexbbq.com

Some say Lexington, a town of twenty thousand with fifteen barbecue places, is the center of the universe for honest-to-goodness barbecue. One of the most famous restaurants is the Lexington Barbecue, where Wayne Monk, locally known as "Honeymonk," serves up pork shoulders, slowly smoked over oak or hickory for at least nine hours. This is one of the original Lexington barbeque places, starting in 1962. They offer a hot, tangy sauce at the table, and their barbecue coleslaw is much like the recipe on page 53. Another popular item is a barbecue salad—lettuce, tomato, and your choice of dressing, topped with chopped barbecue. Hush puppies and unlimited iced tea are featured.

PARKER'S
Three locations in Greenville, North Carolina
(252) 237-0972
parkersbbq.com

In 1946, timbers were floated down the Tar River to build a one-room restaurant. Today it seats 350, but Graham Parker still raises the hogs he barbecues. Whole hogs (weighing 100 pounds dressed) are pit-cooked for 10 hours. Years ago they used oak, but now, with the increased price of wood, they've developed a comparable taste quality using charcoal. For saucing these scrumptious ribs they use a cider vinegar–based mixture with crushed red pepper, black pepper, and salt.

WARD'S BAR-B-CUE
1087 Alice Drive
Sumpter, South Carolina 29150
(803) 775-0008

Five locations within a 120-mile radius of Sumpter. Thad's vinegary, ketchup-base sauce has been in the family for over three generations.

MAURICE'S PIGGY PARK
1600 Charleston Highway
West Columbia, South Carolina 29169
(803) 796-0220
piggiepark.com

At Maurice's Piggy Park, established many years ago, they smoke the pork for 18 hours in a closed hickory pit, seasoning the meat as it smokes. This is definitely a memorable place, combining one of the country's largest drive-ins with indoor service. Now there are 12 locations. They feature three sauces:
Regular: A blend of mustard, apple cider vinegar, soy sauce, peppers, and other spices;
Hickory: Similar to regular, but with added hickory smoke flavoring;
Spicy Hot: With an added dash of extra-hot spices.

CHARLIE VERGOS RENDEZVOUS
52 South Second
Memphis, Tennessee 38103
(901) 523-2746
hogsfly.com

Rendezvous is located downtown in the same basement space off an alley near the Peabody Hotel where it was established in 1948. It has a totally unique underground atmosphere. Their ribs are dry rubbed and basted with a vinegar/water baste, then cooked over charcoal for 2 hours. Before serving, they're seasoned with Charlie's special blend of herbs and spices. A hot, spicy barbecue sauce is served at the table.

Neely's Interstate Barbecue

2265 South Third Street
Memphis, Tennessee 38109
(901) 775-2304
interstatebarbecue.com

Featured on the Food Network, they are a family-style restaurant featuring barbeque everything from nachos to spaghetti and various sandwiches. They possess over 30 years of barbecue experience.

Martin's Bar-B-Que Joint

410 4th Avenue South
Nashville, Tennessee 37201
(615) 288-0880
martinsbbqjoint.com

Martin's has five locations, plus the downtown Nashville location, scattered throughout Tennessee, Kentucky, and West Virginia. They believe in the importance of good technique using the whole-hog approach and live pit barbeque. They make all their sides from scratch and use family recipes for Southern desserts such as pecan and fudge pies and coconut cake.

MIDWEST

CARSON'S
612 North Wells Street
Chicago, Illinois 60654
(312) 280-9200

200 North Waukegan
Deerfield, Illinois 60015
(847) 374-8500

301 West Juneau
Milwaukee, Wisconsin 53203
(414) 223-3311
ribs.com

The ribs at Carson's, which garnered the Spectacular Slab Award from *Chicago Magazine*'s Rib Report years ago, are truly outrageous. They use a sweeter, somewhat Southern-inspired sauce rather than the more frequent tart sauces generally served in the Chicago area. Their baby back ribs are noted for their tenderness and are served with cheesy scalloped potatoes, salt sticks, and onion rolls

SMOQUE IN CHICAGO
125 South Clark Street
Chicago, Illinois 60603
(773) 545-7427
smoquebbq.com

This BYOB restaurant in the Northwest Chicago neighborhood of Irving Park serves on community tables wonderfully smoked dishes of all kinds that has earned a 5-star rating by Zagat. Their meaty St. Louis–style ribs, oak and apple smoked pulled pork, along with lots of traditional 'cue sides are quite popular. Don't forget to try the BBQ Gumbo as well—a homage to Creole cooking that replaces andouille with their own Texas-style smoked sausages. Do be prepared for a wait during peak dining hours as this is some of the finest barbecue in not only Chicago, but the whole country. They have been featured on the Food Network.

Sugarfire Smoke House

605 Washington Avenue
St. Louis, Missouri 63101
(314) 394-1720
sugarfiresmokehouse.com

Multiple locations.

Sugarfire boasts a number of very experienced chefs who have won numerous barbecue awards including the St. Louis Magazine Reader's Choice and Memphis in May awards. They feature innovative dishes such as a Stacked Kraut Ball appetizer and innovative sandwiches such as the Big Muddy. They also offer smoked artichokes, a Chocolate Peanut Butter Bourbon Shake, and claim they use the best local ingredients available to create unconventional, unique, and adventurous flavors.

Pappy's Smokehouse

3016 Olive Street
St. Louis, Missouri 63103
(314) 535-4337
pappyssmokehouse.com

Features Memphis-style barbecue with four different sauces ranging in spiciness and sweetness. Top rated by Zagat, Travel Channel, and the Food Network, they slow roast over fruit woods and specialize in dry rubbed ribs.

Charlotte's Rib

15467 Clayton Road
Ballwin, Missouri
(636) 394-3332
charlottesribbbq.com

A family-style barbecue restaurant! Missouri spare-ribs, beef brisket, and pork steak are cut by hand. Burgoo, very special french fries, American-style potato salad, and sweet-sour coleslaw are side dish specialties.

ARTHUR BRYANT'S
1727 Brooklyn Avenue
Kansas City, Missouri 64127
(816) 231-1123
arthurbryantsbbq.com

Arthur Bryant got started way back in the dust-bowl days of the Great Depression. He loves new customers. "You can get anything at all you want from me, but ya gotta come here and get it!" Arthur Bryant's marvelously smoky ribs are a definite reason to go to Kansas City, Missouri. (They now do take mail orders.)

GATES BAR-B-Q
1325 East Emanuel Cleaver Boulevard
Kansas City, Missouri 64110
(816) 531-7522
gatesbbq.com

Gates Barbecue has six locations and is well known for their sauce. In business for over 60 years, they have mastered their own special flavorful ribs and serve the KC popular Burnt Ends, which are very popular in a sandwich as well as their Sunday Chicken. They are known for being very friendly and informal.

JOE'S KANSAS CITY BARBECUE
3002 West 47th Avenue
Kansas City, Kansas 66103
(913) 722-3366
joeskc.com

Formerly known as Oklahoma Joe's, it has remained constant in the award-winning, painstaking barbecue that it puts out year after year. Owners Jeff and Joy Stehney come out of the ultra-competitive world of the BBQ competition where they perfected the recipes they use today at four locations in and around Kansas City. The original location is a converted gas station and remains home base where you can find locals and BBQ pilgrims alike all chowing down on tender meat bathed in the archetypal sweet and tangy sauce that has come to characterize Kansas City's brand of barbecue. They are known for their burnt ends and succulent ribs. All of their meats are smoked, not grilled. Many say they do not even need the popular sauce as their rubs are so flavorful. *USA Today* rated them as the best barbecue in the country in 2016.

SOUTHWEST

SONNY BRYAN'S
2202 Inwood Road
Dallas, Texas 75235
(214) 357-7120
sonnybryans.com

Run by a very independent, third-generation descendent of an Irishman named Red Bryan, Sonny Bryan's is a small place with school desks for "eatin' in." Operating on a strictly cash basis, he just plain doesn't want to fool with anything other than serving outrageous barbecue. He now has six locations in the Dallas-Ft. Worth area, still serving outrageous barbeque.

LOUIE MUELLER BARBECUE
206 West 2nd Street
Taylor, Texas 76574
(512) 352-6206
louiemuellerbarbecue.com

Located outside Austin, Texas, *Texas Monthly* rated this place as one of the five best in Texas and it won a coveted James Beard Award in 2006. Louie Mueller BBQ has been serving up pit-smoked brisket, massive beef ribs, and sausage (Mueller's own recipe) since 1946. Wayne Mueller is the third-generation owner of this Texas institution, and everything is done according to tradition. When you get to the counter, you are provided with some brisket to snack on while you wait.

BLACK'S BBQ
215 North Main Street
Lockhart, Texas 78644
(512) 398-2712

3110 Guadalupe St.
Austin, Texas 78705
(512) 524-0801
blacksbbq.com

Black's is a Texas tradition in barbecue, family-owned for three generations. Its success and quality has spawned an Austin outpost to go along with the original place in Lockhart, both churning out top notch barbecue. They specialize in slow smoked brisket for 14 hours, house-made sausage (serving an average of 6,000 a week), as well as giant beef ribs (some weighing up to a pound a piece) and smoked pork chops, all smoked with a simple dry rub and local Post Oak wood.

KREUZ MARKET

619 North Colorado Street
Lockhart, Texas 78644
(512) 398-2361
Also locations in Bryan and Bee Cave, Texas
kreuzmarket.com

Kreuz specializes in whole smoked turkeys, sausages, giant beef ribs, brisket, and pork chops. They are one of the original barbeque houses featuring slow smoking with the local Post Oak wood.

SMITTY'S MARKET

208 South Commerce
Lockhart, Texas 78644
(512) 398-9344
smittysmarket.com

The original location for Smitty's was in fact the Kreuz market, which Mr. Schmidt bought in 1948 after working for the market since he was 13 years old. This building is reported to date from early 1924. The original Kreuz concept was continued for smoking the fresh meat that did not sell during the week. Since 1981, the barbeque concept became paramount, leading to a no-frills space with communal tables and a salad bar. Their smoked brisket and pork ribs are their specialties. They are dry rubbed and sauce is only available if requested.

FRANKLIN BARBECUE

900 East 11th Street
Austin, Texas 78702
(512) 653-1187
franklinbarbecue.com

Very promotional-minded owner Aaron Franklin has written a barbecue book and gives BBQ classes in various parts of the world. Noted for the long waits to be served, averaging from 3 to 6 hours—the brisket tends to be everyone's favorite—it is juicy, well rubbed, and blackened when ready to serve.

SALT LICK BBQ

18300 Farm to Market Road 1826
Driftwood, Texas 78619
(512) 858-4959
saltlickbbq.com

The roots of the Salt Lick run back to Mississippi in the mid-1800s. Scott Roberts, who currently owns the Salt Lick, had a great-grandmother who came to the Austin area from Desoto, Mississippi, in 1867, and is credited with founding the place and developing the sauces. Zagat says "This 'landmark' bastion of beef provides a quintessential Texas BBQ experience." They specialize in both pork and beef and have burnt ends as well as turkey and sausage. They have a newer location in Round Rock as well as the Austin Airport.

LA BARBECUE

Aztec Food Park
1906 East Cesar Chavez Street
Austin, Texas 78702
(512) 605-9696
labarbecue.com

Located in a food truck area, La Barbeque is a relative newcomer, established in 2012. However, Zagat's review states that "Just because it's not Franklin's BBQ, doesn't mean it's not worth your time. This is some of the best BBQ in Austin." The brisket is known for literally melting in your mouth.

DANNY'S BARBECUE

1217 East Prospect Avenue
Ponca City, Oklahoma 74601
(580) 767-8304
dannysbbqhq.com

Formerly called Heady Country Barbecue, a few years ago the manufacturing of the sauces and rubs split off and are available both retail and online. Begun in 1986, the restaurant has a large following, with the smoked brisket and ribs being super favorites. They are also known for their baked beans and barbecue-topped baked potatoes.

Mr. Powdrell's BBQ House
11301 Central, North East
Albuquerque, New Mexico 87123
(505) 298-6766
powdrellsbbq.webs.com/

5209 4th ST. NW
Albuquerque, New Mexico 87107
(505) 345-8086

At Powdrell's, ribs are cooked the authentic way—in pits, over hickory wood, maintained at a steady 250°F for ten hours. The sauce, essentially the same as the one developed by Mr. Powdrell's great-great-great-great-grandmother, simmers long and slow. Another location is in an interesting former home at 5209 4th Street, Albuquerque.

Quarters
4516 Wyoming, North East
Albuquerque, New Mexico
(505) 299-9864
quartersabq.com

801 Yale SE,
Albuquerque, NM 87106
(505) 843-6949

The ribs are the big item here. Constantine Nellos, the owner, says they slow smoke their ribs so that they are melt in your mouth. Most agree they are succulent, saucy, and smoked to perfection. When asked about his success, he says, "We really believe in giving high quality with good prices." They also operate a well-stocked liquor store with very competitive prices and feature local wines.

WEST

SMOKE HOUSE BARBECUE & SALOON
424 Sixth Street
Wallace, Idaho 83873
(208) 659-7539
www.smokehousebbqsaloon.com

Set in the old silver mining town of Wallace in northern Idaho in the Bitter Root mountains, the 12-decade-old building built in 1881 is the setting for this barbecue restaurant, which features barbeque and other specialties.

THE BOAR'S NEST BBQ
2008 NW 56th Street
Seattle, Washington 98107
(206) 973-1970
ballardbbq.com

The Boar's Nest features pulled pork, brisket, and ribs in a Southern BBQ style along with the usual sides and standards. It is located in the Ballard area.

PECOS PIT BAR-B-QUE (SO DO)
2260 1st Avenue South
Seattle, Washington 98134
(206) 623-0629
pecospit.com

This is a no-frills lunch place featuring smoke shack style brisket and pulled pork sandwiches, hot links, and beans.

HOLE IN THE WALL
215 James Street
Seattle, Washington 98104
(206) 622-8717
holeinthewallbbq.blogspot.com

This is also a lunch-only place featuring barbecued ribs and chili. They are in a very tucked-away place.

SMOKEY PIT BARBEQUE
160 Harrison Avenue
Auburn, California 95603
(530) 889-9080
smokeypitbarbeque.com

This is a locally very popular place featuring a Texas-style menu with "secret" sauces. A popular item is their barbeque chicken.

BARREL AND ASHES
11801 Ventura Boulevard
Studio City, California 91604
(818) 623-8883
barrelandashes.com

This stylish take on barbecue has been developed by two former French Laundry chefs who had worked for Tom Keller in his highly regarded restaurant. The restaurant features an open hearth, a rotisserie, and a mesquite grill. There is picnic-style eating outside and traditional as well as communal eating indoors. At times there's a long wait to be seated.

PHILIP'S BAR-B-QUE
2619 Crenshaw Boulevard
Los Angeles, California 90016
(323) 731-4772

Also at 4307 South Leimert Boulevard
Los Angeles, California 90008
(323) 292-7613

1517 Centinela Avenue
Inglewood, California 90302
(310) 412-7135

These restaurants feature old-fashioned Southern-style barbeque specialties at great prices. They have many soul food specialties, and their ribs are so succulent, the meat just falls of the bone.

EVERETT AND JONES BARBEQUE

126 Broadway
Oakland, California 94607
(510) 663-2350

4245 McArthur Blvd.
Oakland, California 94619
(510) 698-4380
eandjbbq.com

Everett and Jones is rated highly for their barbeque and generous portions. Many consider their combo plate a huge flavor treat. Their sauces are very popular, and the meats very tender.

KINDERS

1776 Arnold Industrial Way
Concord, California 94520
(925) 825-2333
kindersmeats.com

Kinders now has 13 locations in the Bay Area and one in Reno, Nevada. Begun in 1946, three generations later, they have developed a large following for their barbeque of all kinds and their sauces. The Concord location is their headquarters, which was moved from the original location in San Pablo. They are known for their combination plates, sandwiches, and reasonable prices.

SMOKE BERKLEY BBQ & BEER GARDEN

2434 San Pablo Avenue
Berkeley, California 94702
(510) 548-8801
smokeberkeley.com

This is a Texas-style place with Texans operating it, serving classic barbecue plates and sandwiches. They offer casual dining with the option of outdoor seating. Some favorites are the tea-smoked salmon, ribs, and pulled pork. Their pies are also a favorite.

Sauced BBQ & Spirits

151 Petaluma Boulevard, Suite 129
Petaluma, California 94952
(707) 410-4400
saucedbbqandspirits.com

This more upscale barbecue place features some innovative takes on barbecue such as Brussels sprouts with bacon and loaded potatoes. Though prices are higher than most barbecue places, they are known for generous portions. Favorites are their pulled pork and beef brisket.

INDEX

A

Accompaniments, 51–59
  Barbecued Baked Beans, 55
  Barbecued Cheese, 56
  Chuckwagon Salad, 52
  Corn on the Cob, 56
  Fudge Cake, 58
  Kay's Lexington Barbecue Slaw, 53
  Norma Jean's Hush Puppies, 57
  Texas Pecan Cake, 59
  Texas Potato Salad, 54
Addie's Texas Barbecued Chicken, 45
Alabama Smoky Barbecued Chicken, 24–25
Amy's Sloppy Joes, 41
Anderson, Orin, 3
Anthony's Sicilian Barbecued Chicken, 28
Arthur Bryant's (restaurant), 71

B

Backyard barbecue, 3
Barbecued Baked Beans, 55
Barbecued Cheese, 56
Barrel and Ashes (restaurant), 77
Basics, barbecue, 5–11
  briquettes, 6–7
  cooking meats, tips for, 10
  grills, 5–6
  home smokers, 7–8
  liquid smoke, 10–11
  marinade, 9–10
  roasting temperatures, 11
  sauces, 8–9
  tools, 8
  wood, 8
Basket, hinged wire grill, 8
Basting brush, 8
"BBCs" (Beer Barbecued Pork Chops), 19
Beal, James, 15

Beans, Barbecued Baked, 55
Beef, barbecuing, 10, 21–23, 38–40
  Jerry's, 42
  New Mexico Ribs, 21–22
  "Pulled," 39
  roasting temperature, 11
  Terry Johnson's Hawaiian Luau Ribs, 22–23
  Texas, 40
  Yankee Brisket, Pulled, 38
Beef, ground, see Ground beef
Bernie's Asian Ribs, 35
Big Fish Barbecue, 49
Black's BBQ (restaurant), 72
Blue Smoke (restaurant), 62
Boar's Nest BBQ, The (restaurant), 76
Boyhan, Tom, 37
Branded '72 (restaurant), 64
Brazier grills, 5
Briquettes, see Charcoal briquettes
Brookwood Farms, 27
Brown, David, 18

C

Cake, Fudge, 58
Cake, Texas Pecan, 59
Carnivore BBQ (restaurant), 64
Carson's (restaurant), 69
Carter, Sylvia, 38
Charcoal briquettes, 6–7
  smokers for, 7
  testing, 6
  water smokers for, 7
Charlie Vergos Rendezvous (restaurant), 67
Charlotte's Rib (restaurant), 70
Cheese, Barbecued, 56
Chicken, barbecuing, 24–29, 43–45
  Addie's Texas, 45
  Alabama Smoky, 24–25
  Anthony's Sicilian, 28

Jane's Special Sweet and Sour, 43
Jerry Wood's Personal Favorite, 27
roasting temperature, 11
Southwest BBQ, 29
Sunny Arizona's, 26
Sweet Southern, 44
Chinese smokers, 7
Chuckwagon Salad, 52
Coleslaw, Lexington Barbecue, 53
Corn on the Cob, 56
Country-Style Pork Ribs, 36

D

Danny's Barbecue (restaurant), 74
Date Cream Filling, 58
Down Home Louisiana Barbecued Shrimp, 31–32
Duck, roasting temperature, 11
Dupree, Nathalie, 30

E

Electric grills, 6
Electric smokers, 7
Everett and Jones Barbeque (restaurant), 78

F

Fiery Hot Basting Sauce, 18
Fish Barbecue, 49
   San Francisco, 50
Fletcher's Brooklyn Barbecue (restaurant), 63
Florida Shrimp, 32
Foil tent, making, 25
Fork, 8
Franklin Barbecue (restaurant), 73
Fudge Cake, 58

G

Gas grills, 6
Gas smokers, 7
Gates Bar-B-Q (restaurant), 71
Golden Rule, The (restaurant), 65
Goldstein, Kay, 53
Grills, 5–6

Ground beef
   Amy's Sloppy Joes, 41
   with barbecue sauce, 20
Ground Pork, Barbecued, 34

H

Ham
   Mustard Barbecued Ham, 47
   Orange Barbecued, 46
   Outrageous Steak, 30
Hamburger, *see* Ground beef
Hibachis, 5
Hickory House Pit BBQ, 18
Hinged wire grill basket, 8
Hinterberger, John, 15
Hole in the Wall (restaurant), 76
Home smokers, 7–8
Hush Puppies, 57

J

James Beal's Barbecued Ribs, 15
Jane's Best Barbecued Ribs, 14
Jane's Special Sweet and Sour Chicken, 43
Jerry's Beef Barbecue, 42
Jerry Wood's Personal Favorite Barbecued Chicken, 27
J.K. Wild Boar Soul Barbecue Pit (restaurant), 15
Joeper's Smokeshack (restaurant), 62
Joe's Kansas City Barbecue (restaurant), 71
John Brown's Smokehouse (restaurant), 63
Johnson, Terry, 22

K

Kay's Lexington Barbecue Slaw, 53
Kettle grills, 5
Kinders (restaurant), 78
Kreuz Market (restaurant), 73

L

La Barbecue (restaurant), 74
Lamb, 10
   roasting temperature, 11

Steve's Bermuda, 48
Lexington Barbecue (restaurant), 66
Liquid smoke, 10–11
Louie Mueller Barbecue (restaurant), 72

M

Mandler, Steve, 48
Marinade, 9–10
Martin's Bar-B-Que Joint (restaurant), 68
Maurice's Piggy Park (restaurant), 67
Meat thermometer, 8
Metal spatula, 8
Mighty Quinn's (restaurant), 62
Mitts, oven, 8
Mr. Powdrell's BBQ House (restaurant), 75
Mustard Barbecued Ham, 47

N

Neely's Interstate Barbecue (restaurant), 68
Neil, Florence, 24
Nevada State Chili Contest, 22
New England Maple Barbecued Pork, 37
Newman, Harold, 24
New Mexico Barbecued Beef Ribs, 21–22
Newsday, 38
New York State Pork Cookout, 37
Norma Jean's Hush Puppies, 57

O

Orange Barbecued Ham, 46
Outrageous Ham Steak, 30
Oven mitts, 8

P

Pappy's Smokehouse (restaurant), 70
Parker's (restaurant), 66
Pecan Cake, 59
Pecos Pit Bar-B-Que (SO DO) (restaurant), 76
Pfaffman, Scott, 24
Pfaffman Studios, 24
Philip's Bar-B-Que (restaurant), 77
Pit smoking, 1–2

Pit Stops (restaurants), 61–79
Plant mister, 8
Pork, barbecuing, 10, 14–19, 34–37
    "BBCs" (Beer Barbecued Chops), 19
    Bernie's Asian Ribs, 35
    Country-Style Ribs, 36
    Fiery Hot and South Carolina, 18
    Ground, Barbecued, 34
    James Beal's Ribs, 15
    Jane's Best Ribs, 14
    New England Maple, 37
    roasting temperature, 11
    Super-Secret Baby Back Ribs, 16–17
Potato Salad, Texas, 54
Powdrell's BBQ House (restaurant), 75
"Pulled" Barbecue, 39
Pump spray bottle, 8

Q

Quarters (restaurant), 75
Quayle, Bernard, 3
"Quest for the Best Barbecue in the World, The"
    (Anderson), 3

R

Red Chile Sauce, 22
Restaurants, 61–79
Ribs, barbecuing, 10, 14–17, 21–23, 35–36
    Bernie's Asian, 35
    Country-Style Pork, 36
    James Beal's, 15
    Jane's Best, 14
    New Mexico Beef, 21–22
    Super-Secret Baby Back Pork, 16–17
    Terry Johnson's Beef Hawaiian Luau, 22–23
Rich's Department Stores, 30
Roasting temperatures, 11
Rocklands BBQ and Grilling Company (restaurant),
    64

S

Salad, 52–54
    Chuckwagon, 52

Kay's Lexington Barbecue Slaw, 53
    Potato, Texas, 54
Salt Lick BBQ (restaurant), 74
Sandlapper magazine, 3
San Francisco Barbecued Fish, 50
Sauced BBQ & Spirits (restaurant), 79
Sauces, 2–3, 8–9, *see also specific recipe*
    Fiery Hot, 18
    on hamburgers, 20
    marinade, 9–10
    notes about, 9
    Red Chile, 22
    Sour Cream, 36
    South Carolina, 18
Scott's Bar-B-Que (restaurant), 66
Seattle *Times*, 15
Shrimp
    Down Home Louisiana, 31–32
    Florida, 32
Slaw, Lexington Barbecue, 53
Sloppy Joes, 41
Smitty's Market (restaurant), 73
Smoke Berkley BBQ & Beer Garden (restaurant), 78
Smoke House Barbecue & Saloon (restaurant), 76
Smokehouse barbecuing, 2
Smoke, liquid, 10–11
Smokers, 7–8
Smokey Pig Bar-B-Q, The (restaurant), 65
Smokey Pit Barbeque (restaurant), 77
Smoque in Chicago (restaurant), 69
Sonny Bryan's (restaurant), 72
Sonny's BBQ (restaurant), 65
Sour Cream Sauce, 36
South Carolina Basting Sauce, 18
South Dakota Pork Cookout, 19
Southwest Chicken BBQ, 29

Spatula, metal, 8
Steve's Bermuda Lamb, 48
Sugarfire Smoke House (restaurant), 70
Sunny Arizona's Special Chicken, 26
Super-Secret Baby Back Pork Ribs, 16–17
Sweet Southern Chicken, 44

T

Temperatures, roasting, 11
Terry Johnson's Hawaiian Luau Barbecued Beef
    Ribs, 22–23
Texas Beef Barbeque, 40
Texas Pecan Cake, 59
Texas Potato Salad, 54
Thermometer, meat, 8
Tongs, 8
Tony Romas, A Place for Ribs (restaurant), 63
Tools, 8
Turkey, roasting temperature, 11

W

Wagon grills, 5
Ward's Bar-B-Cue (restaurant), 67
Wood, 8
Wood, Jerry, 27, 42
Wood smokers, 7

Y

Yankee Brisket Pulled Barbecue, 38

Z

Zubke, Bill, 19

www.ingramcontent.com/pod-product-compliance
Lightning Source LLC
Chambersburg PA
CBHW080542110426
42813CB00006B/1184